THIS BOOK BELONGS TO

The Library of

....

....

With so many books out there to choose from, I want to thank you for choosing this one and taking precious time out of your life to buy and read my work. Readers like you are the reason I take such passion in creating these books.

It is with gratitude and humility that I express how honored I am to become a part of your life and I hope that you take the same pleasure in reading this book as I did in writing it.

Can I ask one small favour? I ask that you write an honest and open review on Amazon of what you thought of the book. This will help other readers make an informed choice on whether to buy this book.

My sincerest thanks.

Table of Contents

SUMMARY

The Art of Crochet Produce: Bringing Fiber Food to Life: This book is a comprehensive guide that delves into the intricate world of crocheting fruits and vegetables. This unique and creative craft allows individuals to transform yarn into lifelike replicas of their favorite fiber foods.

The book begins with an introduction to the art of crochet and its history, providing readers with a solid foundation before diving into the specific techniques required to create crochet produce. From selecting the right yarn and hooks to mastering basic stitches, the author takes readers through each step with clear and concise instructions.

One of the highlights of this book is the extensive collection of patterns for various fruits and vegetables. Whether you're looking to crochet a juicy watermelon slice, a vibrant bunch of grapes, or a realistic carrot, this book has it all. Each pattern is accompanied by detailed instructions, stitch diagrams, and full-color photographs, making it easy for both beginners and experienced crocheters to follow along.

In addition to the patterns, The Art of Crochet Produce also includes tips and tricks for adding realistic details to your creations. From creating texture with different stitch patterns to incorporating seeds and stems, the author provides valuable insights that will elevate your crochet produce to the next level.

Furthermore, this book goes beyond just creating individual pieces of crochet produce. It also explores the art of arranging and displaying your creations. Whether you want to create a centerpiece for your dining table or a decorative display for your kitchen, the author offers guidance on how to showcase your crochet produce in a visually appealing and aesthetically pleasing manner.

The Art of Crochet Produce is not just a book for crochet enthusiasts; it is a celebration of creativity and imagination. It encourages readers to explore the possibilities of crochet beyond traditional projects and embrace the joy of bringing fiber food to life. With its detailed instructions, beautiful patterns, and helpful tips, this book is a must-have for anyone interested in the art of crochet and the world of fiber food.

Benefits of Crocheting Your Own Table Decorations: Crocheting your own table decorations can bring numerous benefits and advantages to your home decor. Not only does it allow you to showcase your creativity and personal style, but it also offers a sense of accomplishment and satisfaction. Here are some of the key benefits of crocheting your own table decorations:

1. Personalization: Crocheting your own table decorations gives you the opportunity to create unique and personalized pieces that reflect your individual taste and style. You can choose the colors, patterns, and designs that resonate with you, ensuring that your table decor perfectly complements the overall aesthetic of your home.

2. Cost-effective: Purchasing table decorations from stores can often be expensive, especially if you are looking for high-quality and unique pieces. By crocheting your own table decorations, you can save a significant amount of money. Yarn and crochet hooks are relatively inexpensive, and you can reuse them for multiple projects, making it a cost-effective option in the long run.

3. Therapeutic and Relaxing: Crocheting is known for its therapeutic benefits. The repetitive motions and focus required in crocheting can help reduce stress, anxiety, and even improve concentration. Engaging in this creative activity can provide a sense of relaxation and calmness, allowing you to unwind and escape from the pressures of daily life.

4. Customization: When you crochet your own table decorations, you have the freedom to customize them according to your specific needs and preferences. Whether you want a specific size, shape, or design, you can easily tailor your creations to fit your requirements. This level of customization ensures that your table decorations are not only visually appealing but also functional.

5. Eco-friendly: In today's world, where sustainability is becoming increasingly important, crocheting your own table decorations is an eco-friendly choice. By using yarn and crochet hooks, you are reducing your reliance on mass-produced, often disposable, decor items. Additionally, you can choose eco-friendly yarn options, such as organic cotton or recycled materials, further minimizing your environmental impact.

6. Meaningful Gifts: Crocheted table decorations make thoughtful and meaningful gifts for your loved ones. Handmade items carry a special sentiment and show that you have put time, effort, and love into creating something unique for them. Whether it's for birthdays, holidays, or special occasions, gifting your own crocheted table decorations can leave a lasting impression and create cherished memories.

Gathering Your Crochet Tools and Materials for Crocheting Vegetables:
When it comes to crocheting vegetables, it's important to gather all the necessary tools and materials before you begin. Having everything prepared and organized will make the crocheting process much smoother and enjoyable. So, let's dive into the details of what you'll need to get started.

First and foremost, you'll need a crochet hook. The size of the hook will depend on the type of yarn you're using and the desired outcome of your crochet vegetable. Generally, a medium-sized hook, such as a 4mm or 5mm, works well for most projects. However, if you're aiming for a larger or smaller vegetable, you may need to adjust the hook size accordingly.

Next, you'll need yarn. For crocheting vegetables, it's best to choose a yarn that closely resembles the color and texture of the vegetable you're trying to recreate. For example, if you're crocheting a carrot, opt for an orange yarn with a smooth texture. If you're making a broccoli, choose a green yarn with a slightly fuzzy texture. The possibilities are endless, so have fun exploring different yarn options!

In addition to the crochet hook and yarn, you'll also need a pair of scissors. These will come in handy for cutting the yarn and trimming any excess threads. Make sure to choose a pair of scissors that are sharp and comfortable to hold, as you'll be using them frequently throughout the crocheting process.

To keep track of your progress and make adjustments as needed, it's helpful to have a set of stitch markers. These small, circular markers can be placed on your crochet work to indicate specific stitches or sections. They come in various sizes and colors, so choose ones that are easy to see and won't snag on your yarn.

Another essential tool for crocheting vegetables is a yarn needle. This needle has a large eye and a blunt tip, making it perfect for weaving in loose ends and sewing pieces together. It's important to choose a needle that is compatible with the thickness of your yarn, as a needle that is too small may cause difficulty when working with thicker yarns.

Lastly, consider having a crochet pattern or tutorial on hand. This will guide you through the process of creating your crochet vegetable, providing step-by-step instructions and helpful tips along the way. Whether you prefer a printed pattern or an online tutorial, having a reference will ensure that you stay on track and achieve the desired outcome.

Crochet Stitches for Beginners for Crocheting Vegetables

Crocheting vegetables can be a fun and creative way to add a touch of whimsy to your home decor or even create unique gifts for friends and family. Whether you're a beginner or have some experience with crochet, it's important to have a solid understanding of the fundamental crochet stitches to successfully create crochet vegetables that look realistic and visually appealing.

One of the most basic crochet stitches that beginners should learn is the chain stitch. This stitch forms the foundation of most crochet projects and is used to create a starting row or to add length to a project. It involves creating a series of interlocking loops by pulling the yarn through the previous loop, creating a chain-like structure. The chain stitch is essential for creating the stems or vines of crochet vegetables, as well as for joining different pieces together.

Another important stitch to master is the single crochet stitch. This stitch is used to create tight and dense fabric, making it ideal for creating the body of crochet vegetables. It involves inserting the hook into the stitch, yarn over, and pulling the yarn through both the stitch and the loop on the hook. The single crochet stitch is versatile and can be used to create various textures and shapes, allowing you to bring your crochet vegetables to life.

For more intricate details and textures, the half double crochet stitch is a great stitch to learn. This stitch is slightly taller than the single crochet stitch and creates a looser fabric. It involves yarn over, inserting the hook into the stitch, yarn over again, and pulling the yarn through all three loops on the hook. The half double crochet stitch is perfect for creating the textured surface of vegetables like cauliflower or broccoli, as well as adding depth and dimension to your crochet creations.

If you're looking to create crochet vegetables with a lacy or openwork design, the double crochet stitch is a must-know. This stitch is taller than the half double crochet stitch and creates a more open and airy fabric. It involves yarn over, inserting the hook into the stitch, yarn over again, and pulling the yarn through the first two loops on the hook, then yarn over again and pull through the remaining two loops. The double crochet stitch is great for creating the leaves or petals of crochet vegetables, as well as adding decorative elements to your projects.

Lastly, the slip stitch is a simple yet essential stitch for finishing off your crochet vegetables.

Reading and Understanding Crochet Patterns for Crocheting Vegetables:
Crocheting vegetables can be a fun and creative way to add a touch of whimsy to your home decor or to create unique gifts for friends and family. However, in order to successfully crochet vegetables, it is important to be able to read and understand crochet patterns specifically designed for this purpose.

Crochet patterns for vegetables typically include detailed instructions on the stitches and techniques required to create each individual vegetable. These patterns often include a list of materials needed, such as specific yarn types and colors, as well as the appropriate crochet hook size. It is important to gather all the necessary materials before starting a crochet project to ensure that you have everything you need to complete the pattern.

Once you have gathered your materials, it is time to dive into the crochet pattern itself. Reading and understanding crochet patterns can be a bit daunting at first, especially if you are new to crocheting or have never worked with vegetable patterns before. However, with a little patience and practice, you will soon become familiar with the terminology and symbols commonly used in crochet patterns.

One of the first things to look for in a crochet pattern is the stitch abbreviations. These abbreviations are often listed at the beginning of the pattern and provide a quick reference guide for the different stitches used throughout the pattern. Common stitch abbreviations include single crochet (sc), double crochet (dc), and slip stitch (sl st), among others. It is important to familiarize yourself with these abbreviations to ensure that you are using the correct stitches as indicated in the pattern.

In addition to stitch abbreviations, crochet patterns for vegetables often include special techniques or stitches that are specific to creating realistic vegetable shapes. For example, a pattern for a crocheted carrot may include instructions for creating a textured stitch pattern to mimic the appearance of carrot ridges. These special techniques and stitches add depth and realism to the finished crochet vegetable.

Another important aspect of reading crochet patterns for vegetables is understanding the pattern instructions themselves. Patterns typically include a series of steps or rounds that outline how to create each part of the vegetable, such as the body, leaves, or stem. It is important to read these instructions carefully and follow them in the correct order to ensure that your crochet vegetable turns out as intended.

In addition to written instructions, crochet patterns for vegetables often include visual aids, such as charts or diagrams. These visual aids can be especially helpful for understanding complex stitch patterns or shaping techniques.

Tips for Choosing the Right Yarn and Colors of Crochet Food: When it comes to choosing the right yarn and colors for your crochet food projects, there are a few important factors to consider. The yarn you select will not only affect the overall appearance of your finished piece, but also its durability and texture. Additionally, the colors you choose can greatly impact the realism and visual appeal of your crochet food items. Here are some tips to help you make the best choices for your projects.

First and foremost, consider the type of yarn you want to use. There are various types of yarn available, each with its own unique characteristics. For crochet food projects, it is generally recommended to use a yarn that is soft and washable. This will ensure that your creations are comfortable to touch and easy to clean. Acrylic yarn is a popular choice for crochet food as it is affordable, widely available, and comes in a wide range of colors. It is also durable and easy to care for, making it ideal for items that may be handled frequently.

Another important consideration is the weight or thickness of the yarn. The weight of the yarn will determine the size and density of your crochet stitches. For crochet food, it is typically best to use a medium weight yarn, also known as worsted weight or 4-ply yarn. This weight is versatile and works well for creating realistic textures and shapes. However, if you want to create smaller or more delicate food items, you may opt for a lighter weight yarn, such as sport or baby weight yarn.

In addition to the type and weight of the yarn, the color selection is crucial for achieving the desired look for your crochet food. When choosing colors, think about the specific food item you are trying to replicate. Consider the natural colors and shades of the real food and try to match them as closely as possible. For example, if you are crocheting a strawberry, you may want to choose a bright red yarn for the body and a vibrant green yarn for the leaves. Using variegated yarns can also add depth and dimension to your crochet food, mimicking the natural variations in color found in real fruits and vegetables.

Furthermore, it is important to consider the overall aesthetic you want to achieve with your crochet food. If you prefer a more whimsical or playful look, you can experiment with using bold and vibrant colors that may not necessarily match the natural colors of the food item.

Techniques for Crocheting in the Round for Crocheting Vegetables: Crocheting in the round is a technique that is commonly used in various crochet projects, including the creation of crocheted vegetables. This technique allows you to create seamless and symmetrical pieces, which is particularly important when crafting vegetables that need to resemble their real-life counterparts.

To begin crocheting in the round, you will need a crochet hook and the appropriate yarn for your vegetable project. It is important to choose a yarn that is suitable for the size of your crochet hook and the desired texture of your vegetable. For example, if you want to create a more realistic texture, you may opt for a yarn with a bit of fuzz or a variegated color scheme.

Once you have your materials ready, you can start by creating a slip knot and placing it on your crochet hook. This will serve as the starting point for your round. Next, you will need to make a chain stitch, which will determine the size of your round. The number of chain stitches you make will depend on the size of your vegetable and the desired circumference.

After making the chain stitches, you will need to join the last stitch to the first stitch with a slip stitch. This will create a loop, which will serve as the foundation for your round. From this point on, you will be working in a continuous spiral, without turning your work.

To create the body of your vegetable, you will need to make single crochet stitches into the loop. Insert your hook into the loop, yarn over, and pull up a loop. Yarn over again and pull through both loops on your hook. This will create a single crochet stitch. Continue making single crochet stitches into the loop until you reach the desired height for your vegetable.

To shape your vegetable, you may need to increase or decrease stitches at certain points. Increasing stitches will make your vegetable wider, while decreasing stitches will make it narrower. To increase stitches, simply make two single crochet stitches into the same stitch. To decrease stitches, crochet two stitches together by inserting your hook into the next stitch, yarn over, pull up a loop, then insert your hook into the following stitch, yarn over, and pull up a loop. Yarn over again and pull through all three loops on your hook.

As you continue crocheting in the round, you will notice that your vegetable starts to take shape. You can experiment with different stitch patterns, such as half double crochet or double crochet, to add texture and detail to your vegetable.

Creating Basic Fruit Shapes: Spheres, Ovals, and More of Crochet Food: Creating basic fruit shapes such as spheres, ovals, and more through crochet is a fun and creative way to add a touch of whimsy to your crafting projects. Whether you're looking to make a decorative centerpiece, a keychain, or even a toy for a child, crochet fruit shapes can be a delightful addition.

To begin, you'll need some basic crochet supplies such as yarn, a crochet hook, and a pair of scissors. Choose yarn colors that closely resemble the fruits you want to create. For example, use bright red yarn for apples, yellow for lemons, and orange for oranges. You can also experiment with different shades and textures to add more depth and realism to your fruit shapes.

Start by creating a magic ring, which will serve as the base for your fruit shape. To do this, wrap the yarn around your finger twice, then insert the crochet hook through the ring and pull the yarn through. This will create a loop. Next, chain one to secure the loop and prevent it from unraveling.

To create a sphere shape, you'll need to work in continuous rounds. Begin by single crocheting six stitches into the magic ring. This will form the first round. For the second round, increase each stitch by working two single crochets into each stitch from the previous round. Continue this pattern, increasing the number of stitches in each round until you reach the desired size for your fruit shape.

To create an oval shape, you'll need to work in rows instead of rounds. Start by chaining the desired number of stitches for the length of your oval. Then, single crochet into the second chain from the hook and each chain across. Chain one and turn your work. Repeat this pattern for the desired number of rows, gradually decreasing the number of stitches at each end to create the tapered shape of an oval.

Once you've completed the basic shape of your fruit, you can add details such as a stem, leaves, or even a face if you're creating a toy. To make a stem, simply crochet a small tube shape using a contrasting color of yarn and attach it to the top of your fruit shape. For leaves, crochet a small triangle shape and attach it near the stem. If you're adding a face, use embroidery thread or small buttons to create eyes, a nose, and a mouth.

Crocheting fruit shapes allows for endless creativity and customization. You can experiment with different sizes, colors, and textures to create a wide variety of fruits,…

Texturing Your Crochet for a Realistic Look in Crochet Food: When it comes to creating crochet food, one of the key elements to achieving a realistic look is texturing. Adding texture to your crochet pieces can make them appear more lifelike and visually appealing. In this article, we will explore various techniques and tips for texturing your crochet to give it that realistic touch.

One of the simplest ways to add texture to your crochet food is by using different stitch patterns. Experimenting with different stitches such as popcorn stitch, bobble stitch, or even a simple slip stitch can create interesting textures that mimic the appearance of real food. For example, using a popcorn stitch can give your crochet popcorn a bumpy and textured surface, while a bobble stitch can create the appearance of seeds on a strawberry.

Another technique to consider is using different yarns or yarn weights to create texture. Choosing a yarn with a fuzzy or textured finish can add depth and realism to your crochet food. For instance, using a mohair yarn for crocheting a peach can give it a velvety texture, while using a chunky yarn for a crocheted loaf of bread can create a more rustic and textured appearance.

Additionally, incorporating embellishments can enhance the texture of your crochet food. Adding beads, sequins, or even embroidery can create the illusion of texture and make your crochet food look more realistic. For example, adding small beads to a crocheted cupcake can mimic the appearance of sprinkles, while embroidering small details on a crocheted apple can give it a more textured and lifelike look.

Furthermore, paying attention to color choices can also contribute to the overall texture of your crochet food. Using variegated yarns or blending different shades of the same color can create a more realistic and textured appearance. For instance, using a variegated yarn for crocheting a watermelon can mimic the natural variation in color and texture of a real watermelon.

Lastly, don't forget to consider the shape and form of your crochet food. Adding shaping techniques such as increasing or decreasing stitches can create a more realistic and three-dimensional look. For example, shaping a crocheted carrot with tapered ends can give it a more realistic appearance, while adding curves and contours to a crocheted banana can make it look more lifelike.

In conclusion, texturing your crochet food is an essential step in achieving a realistic look.

Methods for Crocheting Vegetable Shapes

Crocheting vegetable shapes can be a fun and creative way to add a touch of whimsy to your crochet projects. Whether you want to make a cute carrot, a plump pumpkin, or a vibrant tomato, there are various methods you can use to achieve the desired shape and texture.

One popular method for crocheting vegetable shapes is using amigurumi techniques. Amigurumi is a Japanese art of crocheting or knitting small stuffed toys. This technique involves working in continuous rounds to create a seamless and three-dimensional shape. To crochet a vegetable using amigurumi, you would start with a magic ring and work single crochet stitches in a spiral, increasing or decreasing stitches as needed to shape the vegetable. This method allows you to create realistic-looking vegetables with defined curves and contours.

Another method for crocheting vegetable shapes is using tapestry crochet. Tapestry crochet involves working with multiple colors of yarn to create intricate patterns and designs. To crochet a vegetable using tapestry crochet, you would follow a chart or pattern that indicates which color to use for each stitch. This method allows you to create vegetables with detailed textures and patterns, such as the ridges on a pumpkin or the segments on a citrus fruit.

If you prefer a more textured and realistic look, you can use the popcorn stitch or the bobble stitch to create raised bumps or lumps on your crocheted vegetables. The popcorn stitch involves making multiple double crochet stitches in the same stitch and then closing them together to create a raised bump. The bobble stitch is similar but involves making multiple treble crochet stitches instead. By strategically placing these stitches in your crochet work, you can mimic the natural bumps and lumps found on vegetables like broccoli or cauliflower.

To add even more realism to your crocheted vegetables, you can experiment with different yarn textures and colors. For example, using a variegated yarn can create a more natural-looking color variation, while using a textured yarn can add depth and dimension to your vegetables. You can also incorporate other techniques, such as surface crochet or embroidery, to add details like the veins on a leaf or the seeds on a cucumber.

Stitch Variations for Textured Veggie Skins for Crocheting Vegetables: Stitch variations for textured veggie skins in crocheting vegetables refer to different crochet techniques and patterns that can be used to create unique and realistic textures on the surface of crocheted vegetables. These stitch variations add depth and visual interest to the finished product, making them more visually appealing and lifelike.

Crocheting vegetables has gained popularity in recent years as a creative and fun way to incorporate handmade items into home decor, play food sets, or even as props for photography. While the basic stitches like single crochet, double crochet, and half double crochet are commonly used in crocheting vegetables, stitch variations allow crocheters to experiment with different textures and create more realistic-looking vegetables.

One popular stitch variation for textured veggie skins is the popcorn stitch. This stitch creates small raised bumps on the surface of the crocheted vegetable, mimicking the texture of certain vegetables like corn or peas. The popcorn stitch is achieved by working multiple stitches into the same stitch or space and then pulling the loop through all of them at once, creating a raised bump.

Another stitch variation that can be used for textured veggie skins is the bobble stitch. Similar to the popcorn stitch, the bobble stitch creates raised bumps on the surface of the crocheted vegetable. However, the bobble stitch is achieved by working multiple stitches into the same stitch or space and then pulling the loop through all of them at once, but without completing the stitch. This creates a cluster of stitches that forms a raised bump.

In addition to the popcorn and bobble stitches, crocheters can also experiment with other stitch variations like the puff stitch, cluster stitch, or even surface crochet. These stitches can be used to create different textures and patterns on the surface of crocheted vegetables, allowing for endless possibilities in terms of design and creativity.

When using stitch variations for textured veggie skins, it is important to consider the type of vegetable being crocheted and the desired texture. For example, a cauliflower may require a different stitch variation compared to a carrot or a tomato. It is also important to pay attention to tension and gauge to ensure that the stitches are consistent and the texture is evenly distributed.

In conclusion, stitch variations for textured veggie skins in crocheting vegetables offer a wide range of possibilities for creating unique and realistic textures on the surface of crocheted vegetables.

Adding Stalks, Leaves, and Tendrils for Crocheting Vegetables: When it comes to crocheting vegetables, adding stalks, leaves, and tendrils can bring your creations to life and make them look even more realistic. These additional elements add depth and texture to your crocheted vegetables, making them visually appealing and more closely resembling their real-life counterparts.

To start, let's talk about stalks. Stalks are the long, slender parts of vegetables that connect the leaves or tendrils to the main body. They can be crocheted using a thin, elongated stitch pattern to mimic their shape. For example, if you're crocheting a carrot, you can create the stalk by working a series of single crochet stitches in a straight line, gradually decreasing the number of stitches as you move towards the top. This will give the stalk a tapered appearance, just like a real carrot.

Leaves are another important addition to crocheted vegetables. They add a touch of greenery and can be used to enhance the overall look of your creation. Leaves can be crocheted separately and then attached to the main body of the vegetable using a whip stitch or slip stitch. To make the leaves look more realistic, you can use different shades of green yarn and incorporate some shaping techniques. For instance, if you're crocheting a lettuce leaf, you can create a wavy edge by working a combination of single crochet and slip stitches in a pattern that mimics the natural curves of a lettuce leaf.

Tendrils are delicate, curling structures that are often found on vegetables like peas and cucumbers. They can be crocheted using a combination of chains and slip stitches to create a coiled effect. To make the tendrils look more lifelike, you can use a thinner yarn or even embroidery thread to achieve a finer texture. Attaching the tendrils to your crocheted vegetables can be done by sewing them onto the main body using a needle and thread.

Incorporating stalks, leaves, and tendrils into your crocheted vegetables requires attention to detail and a bit of creativity. By carefully considering the shape, color, and texture of these elements, you can elevate your crochet projects to a whole new level. Whether you're making a basket of crocheted vegetables as a decorative piece or creating play food for children, adding these extra features will make your creations stand out and impress anyone who sees them.

Crafting the Perfect Citrus Shape for Crocheting Vegetables: When it comes to crocheting vegetables, one of the most important aspects is crafting the perfect citrus shape. Whether you're making a lemon, lime, or orange, getting the shape just right can make all the difference in the final product.

To start, you'll need to gather the necessary materials. This includes your choice of yarn in the desired citrus color, a crochet hook that matches the yarn weight, and a pair of scissors. It's also helpful to have a tapestry needle for weaving in ends and a stitch marker to keep track of your rounds.

Once you have your materials ready, you can begin by creating a magic ring. This technique allows you to start crocheting in the round, which is essential for achieving a seamless citrus shape. To create a magic ring, simply wrap the yarn around your fingers, insert the hook through the ring, and pull up a loop. Then, chain one to secure the loop and continue with the pattern.

Next, you'll need to work the base of the citrus shape. This is typically done by crocheting a series of single crochet stitches into the magic ring. The number of stitches will depend on the size of the citrus you're making, but a good starting point is usually six to eight stitches. Once you've completed the desired number of stitches, you can pull the tail of the magic ring to tighten the center and close the hole.

From here, you'll begin to shape the citrus by increasing the number of stitches in each round. This is done by working two single crochet stitches into each stitch of the previous round. The exact number of increases will depend on the size and shape you're aiming for, but a common approach is to double the number of stitches in each round. For example, if you started with six stitches in the base, you would have twelve stitches in the next round, twenty-four stitches in the following round, and so on.

As you continue to increase, you'll notice the citrus shape taking form. The number of rounds you'll need to crochet will depend on the desired size and fullness of the citrus. For a smaller fruit, you may only need four to six rounds, while a larger fruit may require eight to ten rounds or more.

Once you've reached the desired size, you can begin to decrease the number of stitches in each round to create the tapered top of the citrus. This is typically done by crocheting two stitches together, also known as a single crochet decrease.

Texturing Techniques for a Realistic Rind for Crocheting Vegetables: When it comes to crocheting vegetables, one of the key elements in achieving a realistic look is the texture of the rind. Whether you're creating a crochet pumpkin, eggplant, or watermelon, the texture of the rind plays a crucial role in making the finished piece look authentic.

There are several texturing techniques that can be employed to achieve a realistic rind for crocheted vegetables. One popular technique is the use of surface crochet. This involves working additional stitches on the surface of the crocheted piece to create raised bumps or ridges that mimic the texture of a real vegetable rind. By strategically placing these surface stitches, you can create the illusion of natural variations in the texture, making the crocheted vegetable look more lifelike.

Another technique that can be used to add texture to the rind is the use of different stitch patterns. For example, using a combination of single crochet and slip stitches can create a bumpy texture that resembles the skin of certain vegetables, such as a cucumber or zucchini. By experimenting with different stitch patterns and combinations, you can achieve a variety of textures that are suitable for different types of vegetables.

In addition to stitch patterns, the choice of yarn can also contribute to the texture of the rind. Opting for a yarn with a slightly rough or textured surface can enhance the realistic look of the crocheted vegetable. Yarns with a tweed or boucle effect can be particularly effective in mimicking the natural texture of vegetable rinds.

Furthermore, adding details such as color changes and shading can further enhance the realism of the crocheted vegetable rind. By using different shades of the same color or incorporating small amounts of contrasting colors, you can create depth and dimension in the rind. Additionally, using techniques such as surface slip stitching or embroidery can add subtle details, such as veins or speckles, that further contribute to the realistic appearance of the crocheted vegetable.

It's worth noting that achieving a realistic rind for crocheted vegetables requires practice and experimentation. It may take some trial and error to find the right combination of techniques, stitch patterns, and yarns that work best for the specific vegetable you're trying to recreate. However, with patience and persistence, you can master these texturing techniques and create crocheted vegetables with rinds that are truly lifelike.

Introduction

When this project was suggested to me, following my first book, I was immediately interested. But this was quite different from my usual plant and animal projects!

Tea parties and imaginary shopping trips are timeless activities that we all have taken pleasure in sharing with our children, nephews, nieces, or grandchildren. What could be more gratifying than offering them a basket of fruits and vegetables that you crocheted yourself! By creating these designs, I was aiming for a result that was cute, colorful, and realistic, with sizes adapted to children. I also wanted to make it possible to put together a cute basket without having to devote months to the crochet work, and to place that basket in your kitchen or on your dining room table as a fun decoration. With just a few exceptions, the designs in this book are fairly quick to complete—with an eye-catching result!

In these pages you will find twenty fruit and vegetable projects (twenty-four, including the variations). I hope that you enjoy crocheting them and offering them to your family and friends—or keep them for yourself!

Apple

Pear

Clementine

Banana

Lemon Half

Raspberry and Blackberry

Cherries

Strawberry

Kiwi Half

Peach, Apricot, and Plum

Eggplant

Peas

Avocado Half

Carrot

Leek

Cauliflower

Radish

Button Mushroom

Pumpkin

Materials

YARN

The designs in this book have been crocheted with DMC brand cotton yarns, chosen for their quality and their availability in stores and online shops.

For each design, you will find the yarn colors and quantities necessary. However, feel free to use the yarn of your choice, of an equivalent weight, or not. If you choose another yarn, you must make sure to use a smaller crochet hook than the one recommended on the yarn ball, so as not to have any gaps between the stitches.

CROCHET HOOKS

The designs in this book were crocheted with four sizes of crochet hooks: 2.5mm (US size B-1 or C-2), 3mm (US size C-2 or D-3), 3.5mm (US size E-4), and 4mm (US size G-6). I have a habit of crocheting tightly, using small hooks. If you are not comfortable with the size recommended, you can certainly use a 3.5mm (US size E-4) crochet hook with DMC Natura Just Cotton Medium. Your finished products will then be a little larger and the stitches a little more spaced apart. If you do that, think about adapting the size of the crochet hook for any other parts of the design (for example: use a 4.5mm crochet hook (US size 7) for the banana peel instead of the 4mm (US size G-6) crochet hook recommended.)

STUFFING

I use polyester stuffing, treated to resist dust mites. It is easy to buy online or in craft stores. You can also find it in yarn shops or fabric stores, or, in a pinch, reuse the stuffing from a pillow! It is difficult to indicate the quantity you will need for each design because it all depends on whether you prefer to stuff lightly or firmly. However, with a 20oz. bag you will be able to make many crocheted fruits and vegetables.

NEEDLES

— Yarn needle and a finer needle to do the embroidery.
— I also find it useful to have long, pointed needles between 3.5in. and 5in. to hide the threads in the stuffing, or to give shape to the fruits and vegetables.

OTHER MATERIALS

— Pins to hold the pieces together when assembling
— Stitch markers: you will need several markers for certain designs. If you don't have any, you can also use a small safety pin, a paper clip, or a short piece of knotted thread on the stitch to be marked.
— Scissors
— Small, flat tweezers, like jewelry tweezers. I often use these tweezers to push in the upper and lower parts of certain fruits and vegetables, or to help me pull a needle through a heavy thickness.

THE BASIC STITCHES

Chain stitch (ch)

1. Make a slip knot: insert the crochet hook in the loop of the knot; then, using the point of the hook, catch the yarn coming from the ball or skein and bring it back through the loop. This slip knot is the starting point, but it never counts as a stitch.

2. To make a chain stitch (ch), yarn over (pass the yarn from back to front, above the crochet hook) and bring this yarn through the loop of the hook.

3. Repeat the second step until you obtain the desired number of stitches. The loop on the crochet hook must never be counted.

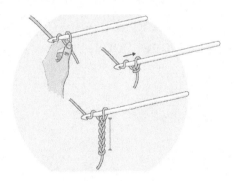

Slip stitch (sl st)

1. Insert the crochet hook in the stitch indicated.

2. Yarn over and bring the yarn through the stitch where the hook is and through the loop on the crochet hook. There should be one loop left on the crochet hook.

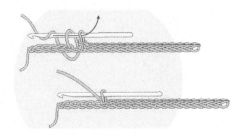

Single crochet (sc)

1. Insert the crochet hook into the stitch indicated.

2. Yarn over and bring the yarn through the stitch where your hook is. There should be two loops on the hook.

3. Yarn over a second time and bring the yarn through the two loops. There should be one loop left on the crochet hook.

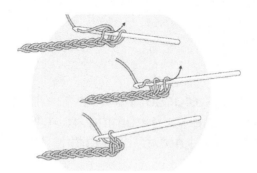

Half double crochet (hdc)

1. Yarn over, then insert the crochet hook into the stitch indicated.

2. Yarn over a second time and bring the yarn through the stitch where your hook is. There should be three loops on the crochet hook.

3. Yarn over one last time and bring the yarn through the three loops. There should be one loop left on the crochet hook.

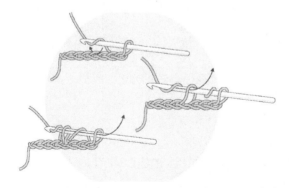

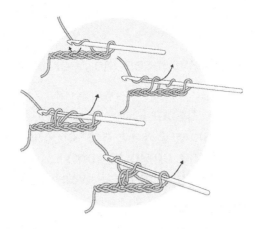

Double crochet (dc)

1. Yarn over, then insert the crochet hook into the stitch indicated.

2. Yarn over a second time and bring the yarn back through one loop. There should be three loops left on the crochet hook.

3. Yarn over a third time and bring the yarn back through two loops. There should be two loops on the crochet hook.

4. Yarn over one last time and bring the yarn back through the two loops. There should be one loop left on the crochet hook.

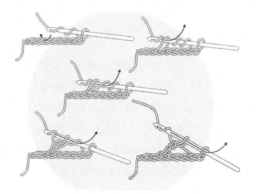

Triple crochet (tr)

1. Yarn over twice, then insert the crochet hook into the stitch indicated.

2. Yarn over a third time and bring the yarn back through the stitch where the crochet hook is. There should be four loops on the crochet hook.

3. Yarn over a fourth time and bring the yarn back through two loops. There should be three loops on the crochet hook.

4. Yarn over a fifth time and bring the yarn back through two loops. There should be two loops left on the crochet hook.

5. Yarn over one last time and bring the yarn back through the two loops. There should be one loop on the crochet hook.

WHERE DO I INSERT THE CROCHET HOOK?

Unless indicated otherwise, always insert the hook from the front to the back.

In a chain
Insert the crochet hook into the upper loops of the chain. At the end of the chain, turn the work to the other side if you are crocheting in rows, or continue crocheting around the end of the chain to form an oval. In this case, continue crocheting on the chain, but this time in the lower loops.

In the stitches of a preceding row
The top of a crocheted stitch always has two small loops forming a horizontal V, no matter what type of stitch you are making. Unless you are told otherwise, always insert the crochet hook under both of these loops.

In the front loop only (FLO)
When this instruction is given, insert the crochet hook only in the front loop—that is, the loop of the V that is closest to you, on the front side of the work.

In the back loop only (BLO)
When this instruction is given, insert the crochet hook only in the back loop—that is, the loop of the V that is farthest from you, on the back side of the work.

CROCHETING IN ROWS

Working in rows always starts with a chain that serves as a base. Crochet from right to left, turning the work (clockwise) at the end of each row. The last stitch crocheted thus becomes the first stitch of the next row. Working in rows makes it necessary to start with one or more chain stitches at the start of each row, depending on the height of the stitches that make up the row (that will be indicated in the instructions for the designs concerned).

CROCHETING IN THE ROUND

Working in the round (rnd) makes it possible to work continuously, without turning the work. Working in the round starts by making a magic circle (or a chain, if you want to make an oval piece), and then you can work in a spiral, or you can close each round with a slip stitch.

Magic Circle
This technique makes it possible to tighten the first round so that there is no gap at the center of the work. Hold the end of the yarn between the thumb and index finger of your left hand. Roll it around your index finger, making one turn. Hold the part of the yarn connected to the ball with the middle finger and the ring

finger. Insert the crochet hook under the loop formed on the index finger (between the yarn and the underside of your finger) and bring back the yarn attached to the ball. Make a chain stitch. The magic circle is ready. Starting from there, crochet the number of stitches indicated in the loop thus formed. All that is left to do is to pull the end of the yarn to tighten the circle. Secure this yarn, if necessary, by crocheting it into the stitches of the second round.

Crocheting in a spiral
This technique consists of crocheting continuously, without closing the rounds.
At the end of a round, simply continue crocheting in the next stitch, which is the first stitch of the round that you just finished.
It is important to use a stitch marker to keep your place in your work. Place this marker on the first stitch of each round. On the last stitch of the round, remove the marker, make the first stitch of the following round, and place the marker over it.

Crocheting in closed rounds
This technique consists of closing each round before moving on to the following one.
After making the last stitch of the round, make a slip stitch in the first stitch that you made at the start of the round. This stitch closes the round, and it is never counted in the stitch count of the round.
To start a new round, first make the number of chain stitches corresponding to the type of stitch that you are going to crochet on this round, to reach the correct height: one chain for single crochet, two for half doubles, three for double crochet, etc. These chain stitches are not counted in the stitch count of the round.
Next, make the first stitch of the new round in the first stitch of the preceding round (the same one as the one in which you just made a slip stitch).
Even though it is easier to keep your place in the work by crocheting in this manner, I suggest that you mark the first stitch of each round in any case.

INCREASES

An increase consists of simply making two stitches in the same stitch of the preceding round or row. The fruits and vegetables essentially are made with single crochet. Also, when you see the abbreviation "inc," this means that you must make two single crochets in the same stitch.

It sometimes happens that you must increase another type of stitch. In this case, the instruction will be "two half double crochets in the same stitch." It may also be necessary to make "three single crochets in the same stitch." Follow the instructions exactly to obtain the expected results.

DECREASES

A decrease consists of crocheting two stitches together to obtain only one stitch in that place. I use the technique of invisible decreases.

When you find the abbreviation "dec," this means that you must crochet two single crochets together. To do that, instead of inserting the crochet hook under both loops of the stitch, insert it in the front loop of the stitch, and then immediately insert it in the front loop of the following stitch. Next make a single crochet.

If you must make a decrease in a half double, follow the same method: yarn over as you would do for a normal half double; then insert the crochet hook in the front loop of the first stitch and immediately afterward in the front loop of the following stitch. Yarn over again, bringing the yarn back through these two front loops. Then yarn over again and bring the yarn back through the three loops on the crochet hook.

COLOR CHANGES

It is important to make a color change at the place indicated in order to obtain the desired result. But to obtain a neat result, you must start at the previous stitch!

To do this, when you crochet the last stitch before the color change, follow these steps:
• Start the single crochet normally. Insert the crochet hook, yarn over, and pull the yarn toward the stitch. You now have two loops on the crochet hook.
• Change the color at that moment by doing a yarn over with a yarn of the new color, and bring this yarn through the two loops on the hook. There is now one loop of the new color on the crochet hook.
• Next, continue to crochet with this new color. Make a knot on the back side of the work with the yarn of the old color and the starting yarn of the new color. I use two techniques, according to the work, as follows:
• When I need to do just a few stitches with another color, and then come back to the main color, I do not cut the yarn of the main color. I hide it in the stitches of the new color; that is, I lay it across the stitches into which I am crocheting, and I crochet normally, hiding the yarn inside the stitches.
• When I need to change color to do a longer length, I make a knot between the two colors of yarn and I cut the yarn. In fact, if you crochet over the yarn, as indicated previously, but over a greater number of stitches and over several rounds, this will create a difference in thickness that will be visible.

FINISHING TECHNIQUES

Clean finishing is very important for an attractive result. Here is how to finish the various parts of the fruits and vegetables.

Finish the yarn invisibly

When you work in a spiral, without closing the rounds, you obtain a sort of stair step. The edge is not clean. To improve this uneven ending, the instructions will ask you to finish with a slip stitch.

Cut the yarn to about 6in. (15cm) and thread a needle with it. Skip over the following stitch and pass the needle under the next two back loops, going from the inside to the outside of the piece. Then pass the needle under the back loop of the slip stitch by inserting it toward the inside of the piece.

Make a knot on the back side of the work.

This technique reproduces the two loops of a stitch above the stitch that you skipped. That makes it possible to obtain a clean result without having to change the number of stitches.

Closing a piece

After making the last stitch, cut the yarn off at about 8in. (20cm). With a needle, pass the yarn under the front loop of the following stitch, from the inside toward the outside. Do the same with all the stitches of the last crocheted round (generally 5 or 6 stitches). Then pull the yarn to close the opening. Pass this yarn through the central hole and bring it out the other side of the crocheted piece. Adjust the tension so that it is well closed, but not enough to crush the piece. Pass the yarn through the piece once or twice more to secure the closure. Cut the yarn flush with the surface of the piece.

ASSEMBLY

Sew two open pieces edge to edge

When the last rounds of two pieces have the same number of stitches, simply pass the yarn from the edge of one piece to the edge of the other, alternating from one stitch of the first piece (from the inside to the outside) to one stitch of the second piece (from the outside to the inside).

Carefully check the alignment after sewing several stitches, and restart if necessary by shifting the first stitch. After joining the last stitches, make several more stitches with the sewing yarn to secure the closure, and then cut it off flush with the piece.

Sew an open piece on a closed piece

These seams are a little more complicated, but you will get better with practice.

Position the piece to be sewn at the desired location and hold it there with pins so that it does not move. You must sew all the stitches of the last round in order to obtain an attractive finish. Insert the needle under a yarn of the closed piece, and then under the two loops of the stitch of the last round, from the inside to the outside.

Repeat this procedure to sew all the stitches. Before sewing the final stitches, add a little stuffing, if necessary. Make several more stitches with the yarn and then cut it off flush with the surface.

OTHER TECHNIQUES USED

Crochet in the third loop of a half double

The half double can be used to create a third loop at the back of the stitch. Insert the crochet hook in this loop to create a distinctive raised relief on the preceding round. The technique is the same as for crocheting in the back loop of a stitch. Just look for this third loop behind the back loop of the stitch and insert your hook in it, from top to bottom.

Embroidery

Several designs have instructions to embroider certain elements. If you know exactly where to place them, you can embroider them before stuffing the piece, and simply make a knot on the back of the work. However, it often is difficult to figure out where to place the design before the piece has been stuffed. To embroider these elements after stuffing, take a long, fine needle and insert it between two stitches, bringing the needle out at the place where you want to embroider. Embroider the elements, and then bring the thread out at the exact spot where it went in at the start. Make a knot with the two threads; then push the knot inside the piece to make it invisible. Using a needle, push the two ends of the thread inside and cut off the extra length.

Running two stitches together

To run two stitches together, insert the crochet hook in the first stitch, yarn over, and bring the yarn back through this stitch. There should be two loops on the crochet hook. Insert the hook in the second stitch, yarn over, and bring the yarn back through this stitch. There are three loops on the crochet hook. Yarn over again and bring back the yarn through these three loops.

ABBREVIATIONS

inc = increase
dc = double crochet(s)
tr = triple crochet(s)
hdc = half double crochet(s)
dec = decrease
st = stitch(es)

sl st = slip stitch(es)
ch = chain stitch(es)
sc = single crochet(s)
row = row
rnd(s) = round(s)
( ) x 6 = crochet item in the parentheses six times
(6 st) = stitch count for each round

SOME ADVICE BEFORE STARTING

To produce smooth work, do not tighten the stitches too much. The crochet hook should be able to pass easily through the stitches, and you should always keep the same tension in your yarn. Do not hesitate to practice making the basic stitches before starting the first design.

Read the instructions for a design completely before starting to make sure that you have understood everything and have not overlooked important information.

WARNING

Important! Certain fruit and vegetable designs in this book are not appropriate for children younger than 3 years of age and present risks of choking. If you make the projects with the yarn indicated in this book, do not leave them within reach of small children, especially the radish, raspberry and blackberry, cherries, peas, and kiwi half.

Apple

Dimensions
Diameter: 2¾in. (7cm)

Important:
The apple is crocheted in a spiral. The stem is crocheted along the starting chain, and the leaf around the starting chain.

Material
› 1 crochet hook, size C-2 or D-3 (3mm)
› DMC Natura Medium Just Cotton (1¾oz.–82yds.) (50g–75m), shade 05, red, or shade 198, light green, ½oz. (15g); shade 11, taupe, 2yds. (2m), and shade 08, green, 2yds. (2m)

STEM

Work in taupe.
Leave 4in. (10cm) of yarn at the start, before the slip knot.
Make a chain of 9 ch, 2 sc in the 2nd stitch starting from the hook, 7 sl st continuing for the length of the chain.
Cut the yarn, leaving about 4in. (10cm) of length.

LEAF

Work in green. Leave 8in. (20cm) of yarn at the start, before the slip knot.
Make a chain of 11 ch, 1 sl st in the 2nd stitch from the hook, then continuing for the length of the chain: 1 sc, 1 hdc, 4 dc, 1 hdc, 1 sc; in the st at the end of the chain: 1 sl st, 1 ch, 1 sl st. Next, crochet the other side of the chain, mirroring the first side: 1 sc, 1 hdc, 4 dc, 1 hdc, 1 sc, 1 sl st.
Cut the yarn, leaving 6in. (15cm) of length.
Using a needle, pass the starting yarn under the last 9 st crocheted, making it come out on the other side of the leaf, alongside the other yarn.

APPLE

Work in red or light green.

Rnd 1: 4 sc in 1 magic circle; do not cut the starting yarn (4 st).

Rnd 2: (1 inc, 1 sc) x 2 (6 st).

Rnd 3: (1 inc, 1 sc) x 3 (9 st).

Rnd 4: 9 inc. (18 st).

Rnd 5: (1 sc, 1 inc, 1 sc) x 6 (24 st).

Rnd 6: (3 sc, 1 inc) x 6 (30 st).

Rnd 7: (2 sc, 1 inc, 2 sc) x 6 (36 st).

Rnd 8: (11 sc, 1 inc) x 3 (39 st).

Using a needle, bring the two yarns of the stem to the inside of the magic circle of the apple; knot them on the inside with the starting yarn of the apple. Do the same thing with the yarns of the leaf, inserting them just beside the stem. Knot the yarns on the inside of the apple by gently pulling on the one that you passed under the st of the leaf, so that it curves a little. It is possible to pull in the cone formed by the first 3 rnds of the apple to make the knots more easily on the inside. Once the stem and the leaf are attached, push the cone back out and continue crocheting.

Rnds 9 to 12: 39 sc (39 st).

Rnd 13: (11 sc, 1 dec) x 3 (36 st).

Rnd 14: 36 sc (36 st).

Rnd 15: (7 sc, 1 dec) x 4 (32 st).

Rnds 16 and 17: 32 sc (32 st).

Rnd 18: (1 sc, 1 dec, 1 sc) x 8 (24 st).

Rnd 19: (1 sc, 1 dec) x 8 (16 st).

Start stuffing. Stuff enough so that the apple is well rounded, but not too firmly, so that you can flatten the top and bottom.

Rnd 20: 8 dec (8 st).

If necessary, finish stuffing.

Work in taupe.

Rnd 21: 8 sc (8 st).

Cut the yarn, leaving 12in. (30cm) of length. Close; then insert a long needle at the center of the apple at the bottom, bringing it out again beside the stem. Insert the needle just alongside, and bring the yarn out again at the bottom. Pull on the yarn to pull in the cones at the top and the bottom; then secure the yarn by taking several stitches in the apple.

Pear

Dimensions
Diameter: 2⅛in. (5.5cm)
Height: 3½in. (9cm)
(without the stem)

Important:
The pear is crocheted in a spiral. The stem is crocheted along the starting chain.

Material
› 1 crochet hook, size C-2 or D-3 (3mm)
› DMC Natura Medium Just Cotton (1¾oz.–82yds.) (50g–75m), shade 99, yellow, ½oz. (15g); shade 08, green, 2yds. (2m)

STEM

Work in taupe.
Leave 10cm of yarn at the start, before the slip knot.
Make a chain of 7 ch, 2 sc in the 2nd st starting from the hook, 5 sl st continuing along the chain.
Cut the yarn, leaving about 4in. (10cm) of length.

PEAR

Work in green.
Rnd 1: 4 sc in a magic circle;
do not cut the starting yarn (4 st).
Rnd 2: 4 inc (8 st).
Rnd 3: (1 sc, 1 inc) x 4 (12 st).
Rnd 4: (1 sc, 1 inc, 1 sc) x 4 (16 st).
Rnd 5: (3 sc, 1 inc) x 4 (20 st).
Using a needle, bring the 2 yarns of the stem to the inside of the magic circle and knot them on the inside with the starting yarn of the pear.
Rnds 6 and 7: 20 sc (20 st).

Rnd 8: (9 sc, 1 inc) x 2 (22 st).
Rnd 9: 22 sc (22 st).
Rnd 10: (5 sc, 1 inc, 5 sc) x 2 (24 st).
Rnd 11: 24 sc (24 st).
Rnd 12: (7 sc, 1 inc) x 3 (27 st).
Rnd 13: (4 sc, 1 inc, 4 sc) x 3 (30 st).
Rnd 14: (2 sc, 1 inc, 2 sc) x 6 (36 st).
Rnds 15 to 19: 36 sc (36 st).
Rnd 20: (2 sc, 2 dec, 2 sc)
Rnd 21: (3 sc, 1 dec) x 6 (24 st).
Start to stuff. Stuff enough so that the pear is well rounded, but not too firmly, so that you can gently flatten the bottom.
Rnd 22: (1 sc, 1 dec, 1 sc) x 6 (18 st).
Rnd 23: (1 sc, 1 dec) x 6 (12 st).
Finish stuffing the pear.
Rnd 24: 6 dec (6 st).
Work in taupe.
Rnd 25: 6 sc (6 st).
Cut the yarn, leaving 12in. (30cm) of length. Close; then, insert a long needle in the center of the pear on the bottom, bringing the yarn out at the center of the pear at the top, beside the stem. Insert the needle again, just beside, and bring the yarn out at the bottom.
Pull to make the bottom cone enter the body of the pear, without flattening the top; then secure the yarn by taking several stitches.

Clementine

⏱ 40 min.

Dimension
Diameter: 1¾in. (4.5cm)

Important:
The clementine is crocheted in a spiral. The leaf is crocheted around a starting chain.

Material
› 2 crochet hooks, B-1 or C-2, and D-3 (2.5mm and 3mm)
› DMC Natura Medium Just Cotton (1¾oz.–82yds.) (50g–75m), shade 109, orange, ¼oz. (8g)
› DMC Natura Just Cotton (1¾oz.–170yds.) (50g–155m), shade 13, green, 2yds. (2m)

LEAF

Work in green using the smaller crochet hook. Leave 4in. (10cm) of yarn at the start, before the slip knot.

Make a chain of 11 ch, 1 sc in the 2nd stitch from the hook: 1 hdc, 3 dc, 2 hdc, 2 sc. In the stitch at the end of the chain, make 1 sl st, 1 ch, 1 sl st. Next, crochet the other side of the chain, in mirror image: 2 sc, 2 hdc, 3 dc, 1 hdc, 1 sc.

Cut the yarn, leaving 6in. (15cm) of length. Using a needle, pass the yarn under 2 loops of the 1 st sc of the leaf, from the back to the front, and then under the back loop of the last sc crocheted. Mark the 2 loops thus formed. Make an invisible knot behind the leaf and pass the yarn under several st before cutting it. Also pass the starting yarn under several st before cutting it.

STEM

Work in green using the smaller crochet hook.
Leave 4in. (10cm) of yarn at the start, before the slip knot.
Make a chain of 9 ch, 2 sc in the 2nd st from the hook, 4 sl st continuing along the chain; make the next sl st by inserting the hook in the marked st on the leaf,

then in the next st of the chain; 2 ch on the remaining st of the chain. Cut the yarn, leaving about 4in. (10cm) of length.

CLEMENTINE

Work in orange using the larger hook.
Rnd 1: 6 sc in 1 magic circle.
Do not cut the starting yarn. (6 st).
Rnd 2: 6 inc (12 st).
Rnd 3: (1 sc, 1 inc) x 6 (18 st).
Rnd 4: (1 sc, 1 inc, 1 sc) x 6 (24 st).
Rnd 5: (7 sc, 1 inc) x 3 (27 st).
Rnd 6: (3 sc, 1 inc, 5 sc) x 3 (30 st).
Rnds 7 to 9: 30 sc (30 st).
Using a needle, bring the yarns of the stem through the magic circle and tie them to the starting yarn of the clementine.
Rnd 10: (3 sc, 1 dec, 5 sc) x 3 (27 st).
Rnd 11: (7 sc, 1 dec, 5 sc) x 3 (24 st).
Rnd 12: (1 sc, 1 dec, 1 sc) x 6 (18 st). Start stuffing.
Rnd 13: (1 sc, 1 dec) x 6 (12 st).
Finish stuffing.
Rnd 14: 6 dec (6 st).
Close and hide the yarn inside.

Banana

Dimensions
Diameter: 1¼in. (3 cm)
Height: 5½in. (14 cm) a spiral to start, and then in rows for the open part.

Important:
The banana is crocheted in a spiral. The peel is crocheted in

Material
› 2 crochet hooks, C-2 or D-3, and G-6 (3mm and 4mm)
› DMC Natura Medium Just Cotton (1¾oz.–82yds.) (50g–75m), shade 03, off white, ½oz. (15g); shade 09, yellow, ¾oz. (17g); and shade 02, black, 2yds. (2m)

BANANA

Work in off-white using the smaller crochet hook. Stuff lightly as you go along.
Rnd 1: 6 sc in 1 magic circle (6 st).
Rnd 2: (1 inc, 2 sc) x 2 (8 st).
Rnd 3: (1 sc, 1 inc) x 4 (12 st).
Rnd 4: (1 sc, 1 inc, 1 sc) x 4 (16 st).
Rnds 5 to 26: 16 sc (16 st).
Rnd 27: (1 sc, 1 dec, 1 sc) x 4 (12 st).
Rnd 28: 6 dec. (6 st).
Cut the yarn, leaving 16in. (40 cm) of length. Close; then, using a needle, insert the needle along an imaginary line that would join the 2 ends of the banana. Do not run the needle through the stuffing, but just under the stitches.
Gently pull the yarn to curve the banana slightly, take several stitches to secure the yarn. Cut the yarn close to the surface.

PEEL

Crochet this part loosely with the larger crochet hook.
Work in black.
Rnd 1: 6 sc in a magic circle (6 st).

Work in yellow.
Rnd 2: 6 sc in the back loop only (6 st).
Rnd 3: (1 sc, 1 inc) x 3 (9 st).
Rnd 4: (1 ms, 1 inc, 1 sc) x 3 (12 st).
Tie a knot and pull the starting yarns inside.
Rnd 5: (1 sc, 1 inc) x 6 (18 st).
Rnds 6 to 16: 18 sc (18 st).
Starting from now, crochet the 3 peel sections in rows, one after the other.

1st Peel section
Row 1: 6 sc in the first 6 st of rnd 16, turn (6 st).
Rows 2 to 8: 1 ch, 6 sc, turn (6 st).
Row 9: 1 ch, 1 sc, run 2 st together, 3 sc, turn (5 st). For more instructions on running 2 st together, see the "Techniques" chapter, p. 29.
Row 10: 1 ch, 5 sc, turn (5 st).
Row 11: 1 ch, 2 sc, run 2 st together, 1 sc, turn (4 st).
Row 12: 1 ch, 4 sc, turn (4 st).
Row 13: 1 ch, 1 sc, run 2 st together, 1 sc, turn (3 st).
Row 14: 1 ch, 3 sc, turn (3 st).
Row 15: 1 ch, run 3 st together (1 st).
To come back down the edge of the peel section, make 13 sc up to the 6th st of row 1, 1 sl st in the 6th st of rnd 16.

2nd Peel section
Row 1: 6 sc in the next 6 st of rnd 16 (st 7 to 12), turn (6 st).
Rows 2 to 15: Follow the instructions for the 1st peel section.

3rd Peel section
Row 1: 6 sc in the next 6 st of rnd 16 (st 13 to 18), turn (6 st).
Rows 2 to 15: Follow the instructions for the 1st peel section.
To come back down the edge of the peel section, make 13 sc up to the 6th st of row 1, 1 sl st in the 18th st of rnd 16.
Tie a knot in the yarn on the inside of the peel and bring the yarn to the inside.
To insert the banana into its peel, pull the peel apart a little with your fingers.

Lemon

Dimensions
Diameter: 2in. (5cm)
Length: 3⅓in. (8.5cm)

Important:
The lemon is crocheted in a spiral.

Material
› 1 crochet hook, size C-2 or D-3 (3mm)
› DMC Natura Medium Just Cotton (1¾oz.–82yds.) (50g–75m), shade 99, yellow, ½oz. (15g); shade 08, green, 2yds. (2m)

LEMON

Work in green.
Rnd 1: 6 sc in 1 magic circle (6 st).
Work in yellow.
Rnd 2: 6 sc (6 st).
Rnd 3: (1 inc, 1 sc) x 3 (9 st).
Rnd 4: 9 inc (18 st).
Rnd 5: (4 sc, 1 inc, 1 sc) x 3 (21 st).
Rnd 6: (1 sc, 1 inc, 5 sc) x 3 (24 st).
Rnd 7: (7 sc, 1 inc) x 3 (27 st).
Rnd 8: (3 sc, 1 inc, 5 sc) x 3 (30 st).
Rnds 9 to 13: 30 sc (30 st).
Rnd 14: (8 sc, 1 dec) x 3 (27 st).
Rnd 15: 27 sc (27 st).
Rnd 16: (3 sc, 1 dec, 4 sc) x 3 (24 st).
Start stuffing.
Rnd 17: (5 sc, 1 dec, 1 sc) x 3 (21 st).
Rnd 18: (1 sc, 1 dec, 4 sc) x 3 (18 st).
Rnd 19: (1 sc, 1 dec) x 6 (12 st).
Continue stuffing.
Rnd 20: 6 dec (6 st).

Rnd 21: 6 sc (6 st).
Close and pull the yarn to the inside.

Lemon Half

Dimensions
Diameter: 2in. (5cm)
Height: 1¾in. (4.5cm)

Important:
The lemon half is crocheted in a spiral. The slice is crocheted in closed rounds. The sl st that closes each round and the ch that starts each rnd are not indicated for reasons of readability, **but they must be done for each round**. For more instructions, see the "Techniques" chapter.

Material
> 1 crochet hook, size C-2 or D-3 (3mm)
> DMC Natura Medium Just Cotton (1¾oz.–82yds.) (50g–75m), shade 99, yellow, ¼oz. (8g); shade 09, light yellow, ⅛oz. (2g); shade 08, green, 2yds. (2m); and shade 01, white, 3yds. (3m).
> DMC Natura Just Cotton (1¾oz.–170yds.) (50g–155m), shade 01, white, 1yd. (1m)

LEMON HALF

Crochet rnds 1 to 10 according to the instructions for the entire lemon.
Rnd 11: 29 sc, 1 sl st (30 st).
Cut the yarn, leaving 24in. (60cm) of length.
Using a yarn needle, pass the yarn under the 2 loops of the following st, from the inside to the outside. Next, pass the yarn under the **back loop only** of the preceding st (last st of rnd 11), from the outside to the inside. In doing that, a 31st st has been created. End by passing the yarn under the **back loop only** of this st, from the outside to the inside. Do not cut.

SLICE

Work in light yellow.
Rnd 1: 6 sc in 1 magic circle (6 st).
Rnd 2: 6 inc (12 st).

Rnd 3: (1 sc, 1 inc) x 6 (18 st)
Rnd 4: (1 sc, 1 inc, 1 sc) x 6 (24 st).
In white (medium yarn).
Rnd 5: (3 sc, 1 inc) x 6 (30 st).
Close invisibly as follows:
Using a yarn needle, pass the yarn under the 2 loops of the 1st st of the rnd, from the inside to the outside. Next, pass the yarn under the **back loop only** of the preceding st (last st of rnd 5), from the outside to the inside.
Make a knot behind and cut. A 31st st has been created.
With the fine white yarn, embroider 6 sections in a star shape by passing through the starting magic circle each time, and on the outside of the 4th rnd of the slice.

ASSEMBLY

Using the yellow yarn of the lemon half, sew the two parts together, passing the yarn through both loops of the slice, from the top toward the bottom, and **only in the back loop** of the lemon half, from the inside toward the outside. Before doing the last stitches, stuff the lemon half. Bring the yarn to the inside and cut it.
To finish, in yellow, pull a yarn through the **front loop** of one of the stitches of rnd 11 of the lemon half; crochet 31 sc all around using the **front loop** of the stitches.
Then crochet 31 sl st all around.
Bring the starting and ending yarns to the inside and clip.

Raspberry and Blackberry

🕐 30 min.

Dimensions
Diameter: 1¼in. (3cm)

Important:
All the elements are crocheted in a spiral. To give a slightly different surface texture to the raspberry (or blackberry) stitches, I crochet the sc differently. I modify the 2 yarnovers of each sc by passing the yarn under the hook, from back to front, instead of passing it over the crochet hook. If you are not comfortable doing this, you can make the sc normally. The leaves and the stem are crocheted by doing the yarnovers normally.

Material
› 2 crochet hooks, B-1 or C-2, and D-3 (2.5mm and 3mm)
› DMC Natura Medium Just Cotton (1¾oz.–82yds.) (50g–75m); **for the raspberry:** shade 444, rose, 5yds. (5m); **for the blackberry:** shade 126, violet, 5yds. (5m)
› DMC Natura Just Cotton (1¾oz.–170yds.) (50g– 155m), shade 76, green, 2yds. (2m)

RASPBERRY AND BLACKBERRY

Work in rose or violet, using the larger crochet hook.
Crochet rnds 2 to 7 in the **front loop** of the st.
Rnd 1: 5 sc in 1 magic circle (5 st).
Rnd 2: 5 inc (10 st).
Rnd 3: 10 sc (10 st).
Rnd 4: (1 sc, 1 inc) x 5 (15 st).
Rnd 5: 15 sc (15 st).
Rnd 6: (1 sc, 1 inc, 1 sc) x 5 (20 st).
Rnd 7: 10 dec (10 sc).
Stuff.
Rnd 8: 5 dec (5 st).
Cut the yarn, leaving 8in. (20cm) of length.

Close; then, using a needle, pass through the center of the raspberry (or blackberry) with this yarn, top to bottom, coming out in the middle of the starting magic circle. Pull on the yarn to flatten the height of the berry. Take a few more stitches to secure the yarn, then cut it.

LEAVES

Work in green using the smaller crochet hook.
Rnd 1: 5 sc in 1 magic circle. Do not cut the starting yarn (5 st).
Rnd 2: 1 sl st, (4 ch, 1 sc in the 2nd st from the hook, then continuing along the chain: 1 sl st, 1 sc; 1 sl st in the next st on rnd 1) x 5. The 5th time, make the last sc above the 1st sc of rnd 2.
Cut the yarn, leaving 12in. (30cm) of length.

STEM

Work in green using the smaller crochet hook.
Make 1 chain of 3 ch, keeping 4in. (10cm) of yarn before the starting slip knot, 1 sc in the 2nd st from the hook, 1 sc in the next st.
Cut the yarn, leaving 4in. (10cm) of length.

ASSEMBLY

Sew the stem to the leaves by bringing the yarns of the stem in through the magic circle and tying them behind the starting yarn of the leaves.
Then sew the leaves to the top of the berry. Sew only the central round so that the ends of the leaves remain free.

Cherries

🕐 1 hr.

Dimensions
Diameter: 1¼in. (3cm)
Height: 3in. (8cm)

Important:
The cherries are crocheted in a spiral. The stem is crocheted along a starting chain and the leaf is crocheted around a chain.

Material
› 1 crochet hook, size B-1 or C-2 (2.5mm)
› DMC Natura Just Cotton (1¾oz.–170yds.) (50g–155m), shade 76, green, 2yds. (2m); shade 23, red, ¼oz. (6g).

STEM

Work in green. Keep 4in. (10cm) of yarn at the start, before the slip knot.
Make one chain of 23 ch, 1 sl st in the 2nd ch from the hook, 3 sl st in the following ch, 18 ch.
Cut the yarn, leaving 4in. (10cm) of length.

CHERRY × 2

Work in red.
Rnd 1: 6 sc in the magic circle. Do not cut the starting yarn. (6 st).
Rnd 2: (1 inc, 1 sc) x 3 (9 st).
Rnd 3: 9 sc (9 st).
Rnd 4: 9 inc (18 st).
Rnd 5: (1 sc, 1 inc, 1 sc) x 6 (24 st).
Rnd 6: (7 sc, 1 inc) x 3 (27 st).
Using a needle, bring one of the ends of the stem through the starting magic circle of the cherry, from the outside toward the inside.
Tie a knot in the starting red yarn.
Rnds 7 to 9: 27 sc (27 st).

Rnd 10: (7 sc, 1 dec) x 3 (24 st).
Rnd 11: (3 sc, 1 dec, 3 sc) x 3 (21 st).
Rnd 12: (5 sc, 1 dec, 3 sc) x 3 (18 st).
Stuff enough so that the cherry is rounded, but not too firmly, so that you will be able to flatten the top afterward.
Rnd 13: (1 sc, 1 dec) x 6 (12 st).
If necessary, finish stuffing.
Rnd 14: 6 dec (6 st).
Cut the yarn, leaving 8in. (20cm) of length.
Close, and then, using a needle, cross the cherry with this yarn from the top and bring the yarn out at the middle of the starting magic circle.
Pull on the yarn to flatten the top of the cherry a bit.
Take another stitch or two with the yarn to secure the yarn, then cut it.

LEAF

Work in green.
Make a chain of 15 ch, leaving 6in. (15cm) of yarn at the start, 1 sc in the 2nd st from the hook, and then continuing along the chain: 1 sc, 1 hdc, 2 dc, 4 tr, 2 dc, 1 hdc, 1 sc; in the st at the end of the chain: 1 sc, 1 ch, 1 sc; come back down the other side, mirroring the first side: 1 sc, 1 hdc, 2 dc, 4 tr, 2 dc, 1 hdc, 1 sc, 1 sl st.
Using the same yarn, make 3 sc in the doubled part of the stem, where you will attach the leaf. Make the 1st sc in the st just above the place where the two stems separate, then make the next two in the 2 st above (it is the front loop of ch 19 to 21 of the stem chain).
Cut the yarn, leaving 6in. of length.
Tie a simple knot at the top of the stem and bring the yarn back through the top 4 st.
Using a needle, bring the starting yarn of the leaf under the stitches, along the midline, and then cut it off flush with the stem.

Strawberry

Dimensions
Height: 1¾in. (4.5cm)

Important:
The strawberry and the leaves are crocheted in a spiral. The stem is crocheted along the starting chain.

Material
› 2 crochet hooks, size B-1 or C-2 (2.5mm), and size C-2 or D-3 (3mm)
› DMC Natura Medium Just Cotton (1¾oz.–82yds.) (50g–75m), shade 55, red, 11yds. (10m)
› DMC Natura Just Cotton (1¾oz.–170yds.) (50g–155m), shade 48, green, 3¼yds. (3m), and shade 01, white, 1yd. (1m)

STRAWBERRY

Work in red using larger crochet hook.
Rnd 1: 5 sc in the magic circle (5 st).
Rnd 2: 5 inc (10 st).
Rnd 3: 10 sc (10 st).
Rnd 4: (1 sc, 1 inc) x 5 (15 st).
Rnd 5: 15 sc (15 st).
Rnd 6: (1 sc, 1 inc, 1 sc) x 5 (20 st).
Rnd 7: 20 sc (20 st).
Rnd 8: (2 sc, 1 inc, 2 sc) x 4 (24 st)
Rnds 9 and 10: 24 sc (24 st).
Rnd 11: 12 dec (12 st).
Stuff.
Rnd 12: 6 dec (6 st).
Cut the yarn, leaving 12in. (30cm) of length.
Close, then, using a needle, pass the yarn through the strawberry lengthwise and bring the yarn out through the middle of the starting magic circle.
Pull on the yarn to flatten the top of the strawberry a little. Do another stitch or two with the yarn to secure it, then cut it.

Using a fine needle and fine white yarn, embroider small vertical lines randomly over the entire strawberry.

LEAVES

Work in green using the smaller crochet hook.
Rnd 1: 7 sc on the magic circle.
Do not cut the starting yarn (7 st).
Rnd 2: 1 sl st, (6 ch, 1 sl st in the 2nd st from the hook, then continuing along the chain: 1 sl st, 3 sc; 1 sl st in the next st on Rnd 1) x 7. The 7th time, make the last sl st above the 1 st sl st of Rnd 2.
Cut the yarn, leaving 12in. (30cm) of length.

STEM

Work in green using the smaller crochet hook.
Make a chain of 4 ch, leaving 4in. (10cm) of yarn before the starting slip knot, 1 sl st in the 2nd st from the hook, 1 sl st in the next 2 st.
Cut the yarn, leaving 4in. (10cm) of length.

ASSEMBLY

Sew the stem to the leaves by passing the yarn of the stem through the starting magic circle and tie a knot on the back side using the starting yarn of the leaves. Then sew the leaves to the top of the strawberry. Sew only the central round at the base of the leaves, so that the extremities of the leaves remain free.

Kiwi Half

Dimensions
Diameter: 1¾in. (4.5cm)
Height: 1¼in. (3cm)

Important:
The kiwi half is crocheted in a spiral. The slice is crocheted in the round, in closed rounds. To keep the instructions easy to follow, the sl st that closes each round and the ch that starts each round are not indicated, **but they must be done at every round**. For more instructions, see the "Techniques" chapter.

Material
›   1 crochet hook, size C-2 or D-3 (3mm)
›   DMC Natura Medium Just Cotton (1¾oz.–82yds.) (50g–75m), shade 89, brown, ¼oz. (7g); shade 198, green, ⅛oz. (2g); and shade 01, white, 1yd. (1m)
›   DMC Pearl Cotton, black, about 1yd. (1m)

KIWI HALF

Work in brown.
Rnd 1: 6 hdc in 1 magic circle (6 st).
Rnd 2: 6 inc in the **3rd loop** of the hdc of the preceding rnd (for more instructions see the "Techniques" chapter, (12 st).
Rnd 3: (1 sc, 1 inc) x 6 (18 st).
Rnd 4: (4 sc, 1 inc, 1 sc) x 3 (21 st).
Rnd 5: (1 sc, 1 inc, 5 sc) x 3 (24 st).
Rnd 6: 24 sc (24 st).
Rnd 7: (3 sc, 1 inc, 4 sc) x 2, 3 sc, 1 inc, 3 sc, 1 sl st (27 st).
Cut the yarn, leaving 24in. (60cm) of length.
Skip 1 st and, using a yarn needle, pass the yarn under the 2 loops of the following st, from the inside to the outside. Next pass the yarn under the **back loop only** of the preceding st (last st of rnd 7), from the outside to the inside.

End by passing the yarn under the **back loop only** of the st that you have just made above the 1st st of rnd 7, from the outside to the inside. Do not cut.

SLICE

Work in white.
Rnd 1: 6 sc in 1 magic circle (6 st).
Work in green.
Rnd 2: 6 inc (12 st).
Rnd 3: (1 sc, 1 inc) x 6 (18 st).
Rnd 4: (1 sc, 1 inc) x 9 (27 st).
Close invisibly.
Using the black pearl cotton, embroider small black lines all around the central white round, crossing rnd 2.

ASSEMBLY

Using the brown yarn of the kiwi half, sew the 2 parts together, inserting the needle under both loops of the slice, from the top to the bottom, and **only in the back loop** of the kiwi half, from the inside to the outside.
Before doing the last stitches, stuff the kiwi half.
Pull the yarn to the inside and clip.
To finish, in brown, pull a yarn into the front loop of one of the st of rnd 7 of the kiwi half, and make 27 sc all around in the **front loop** of the stitches.
Then make 27 sl st all around.
Pull the starting and ending yarns to the inside and clip.

Peach, Apricot, and Plum

⏱ 45 min.

Dimensions
Diameter: 2⅛in. (5.5cm)

Important:
Complete instructions are given for the peach. To make the apricot or the plum, see the slight modifications, printed after the instructions for the peach. The peach is crocheted in a spiral. The stem is crocheted along a starting chain, and the leaf is crocheted around a starting chain.

Material
› 2 crochet hooks, size B-1 or C-2 (2.5mm), and size C-2 or D-3 (3mm)
› DMC Natura Medium Just Cotton (1¾oz.–82yds.) (50g–75m), **for the peach:** shade 310, blush, ½oz. (12g); **for the apricot:** shade 10, apricot, ½oz.; **for the plum:** shade 126, violet, ½oz.; for all three: shade 89, brown, 2yds. (2m).
› DMC Natura Just Cotton (1¾oz.—170yds.) (50g–155m), shade 76, green, 2yds. (2m)

STEM

Work in brown using the larger crochet hook. Leave 4in. (10cm) of starting yarn, before the slip knot.
Make a chain of 5 ch, 1 sc in the 2nd st from the hook, 3 sl st continuing along the chain.
Cut the yarn, leaving about 4in. of length.

LEAF (OPTIONAL)

Work in green using the smaller crochet hook. Leave 6in. (15cm) of starting yarn, before the slip knot.
Make 1 chain of 10 ch, 1 sc in the 2nd st from the hook; continuing along the chain: 1 hdc, 1 dc, 2 tr, 1 dc, 1 hdc, 1 sc; in the st at the end of the chain:
1 sl st, 1 ch, 1 sl st; then crochet in mirror image on the other side of the chain: 1 sc, 1 hdc, 1 dc, 2 tr, 1 dc, 1 hdc, 1 sc.

Cut the yarn, leaving about 4in. of length.
Using a needle, thread the starting yarn under the last 8 st crocheted, coming out at the other side of the leaf, beside the other yarn.

PEACH

Work in blush using the larger crochet hook.
Leave about 12in. (30cm) of length of yarn at the starting magic circle and do not cut it.
Rnd 1: 4 sc in 1 magic circle (4 st).
Rnd 2: (1 inc, 1 sc) x 2 (6 st).
Rnd 3: 1 sc in the **back loop only**, 1 inc, (1 sc, 1 inc) x 2 (9 st).
Rnd 4: 1 inc in the **back loop only**, 8 inc (18 st).
Rnd 5: 1 sc in the **back loop only**, 1 inc, 1 sc, (1 sc, 1 inc, 1 sc) x 5 (24 st).
Rnd 6: 1 sc in the **back loop only**, 1 inc, 1 sc, (1 sc, 1 inc, 1 sc) x 7 (32 st).
Using a needle, bring 2 of the yarns of the stem to the inside of the magic circle and tie them on the inside to the starting yarn of the peach.
You can push the cone formed by the first 3 rnds in to make it easier to tie the knots on the inside.
Once the stem is attached, push the cone back out. If you wish to add a leaf, attach it in the same way, by pushing the hook through just beside the stem.
Using a yarn needle, bring the peach starting yarn through the magic circle to the outside of the peach, then under the front loops of the 1st st of rnds 3 to 5.
Leave the yarn there and continue to crochet.
Rnds 7 to 13: 1 sc in the **back loop only**, 31 sc (32 st).
Rnd 14: 1 sc in the **back loop only**, 1 dec, 1 sc (1 sc, 1 dec, 1 sc) x 7 (24 st).
Rnd 15: 1 sc in the **back loop only**, 1 dec, 1 sc, (1 sc, 1 dec, 1 sc) x 5 (18 st).
Start to stuff. Stuff enough for the peach to be well rounded, but not too firmly, so that you will be able to flatten the top and the bottom and the vertical crease.
Rnd 16: 1 sc in the **back loop only**, 1 dec, (1 sc, 1 dec) x 5 (12 st).
If necessary, finish stuffing.
Rnd 17: 1 sc in the **back loop only**, 5 dec, 1 sc (7 st).
In brown.
Rnd 18: 1 sc in the **back loop only**, 6 sc (7 st).
Cut the brown yarn, leaving 12in. (30cm) of length.
Close; then, push a long needle in at the center of the peach on the bottom, and bring the yarn out of the center of the peach at the top, beside the stem. Push the needle back in just alongside, and bring it out again at the bottom. Pull to bring the top and bottom cones inward, then secure the yarn by taking another stitch.

Thread the waiting blush yarn through a yarn needle and pass it under the 1st st of the remaining rnds (rnds 6 to 17). Push the needle in close to the center at the bottom of the peach and bring the yarn out again at the center top. Pull on the yarn to create a vertical crease, along the line of the 1st st of each rnd. Secure the yarn by taking another stitch or two.

APRICOT

Follow the same steps as for the peach, using the apricot yarn, making only the following changes:
Rnd 6: 1 sc in the **back loop only**, 4 sc, 1 inc, (5 sc, 1 inc) x 3 (28 st).
Rnds 7 to 13: 1 sc in the **back loop only**, 27 sc (28 st).
Rnd 14: 1 sc in the **back loop only**, 4 sc, 1 dec, (5 sc, 1 dec) x 3 (24 st).
Then follow rnds 15 to 18 of the peach.
Rnd 18: Use the apricot yarn instead of the brown.

PLUM

Follow the same steps as for the peach, using the violet yarn, making only the following changes:
Rnd 6: 1 sc in the **back loop only**, 4 sc, 1 inc, (5 sc, 1 inc) x 3 (28 st).
Rnds 7 to 14: 1 sc in the **back loop only**, 27 sc. (1 rnd more than for the apricot) (28 st).
Rnd 15: 1 sc in the **back loop only**, 4 sc, 1 dec, (5 sc, 1 dec) x 3 (24 st).
Start to stuff. Stuff enough for the peach to be well rounded, but not too firmly, so that you will be able to flatten the top and the bottom and the vertical crease.
Then follow rnds 16 to 18 of the peach, crocheting the last rnd in violet instead of brown.

Tomato

Dimensions
Diameter: 2⅛in. (5.5cm)

Important:
All the elements are crocheted in a spiral.

Material
› 2 crochet hooks, size B-1 or C-2 (2.5mm), and size C-2 or D-3 (3mm)
› DMC Natura Medium Just Cotton (1¾oz.–82yds.) (50g–75m), shade 55, red, ⅓oz. (10g)
› DMC Natura Just Cotton (1¾oz.–170yds.) (50g–155m), shade 48, green, 2yds. (2m)

TOMATO

Work in red using the larger crochet hook.
Rnd 1: 6 sc in a magic circle (6 st).
Rnd 2: (1 inc, 1 sc) x 3 (9 st).
Rnd 3: (1 sc, 1 inc, 1 sc) x 3 (12 st).
Rnd 4: 12 inc (24 st).
Rnd 5: [2 sc, (1 sc, 1 inc) x 2, (1 inc, 1 sc) x 2, 2 sc] x 2 (32 st).
Rnds 6 to 11: 32 sc (32 st).
Rnd 12: [2 sc, (1 sc, 1 dec) x 2, (1 dec, 1 sc) x 2, 2 sc] x 2 (24 st).
Rnd 13: (1 sc, 1 dec, 1 sc) x 6 (18 st).
Stuff enough so that the tomato is well rounded, but not too firm.
Rnd 14: (1 sc, 1 dec) x 6 (12 st).
Finish stuffing.
Rnd 15: 6 dec (6 st).
Cut the yarn, leaving 12in. (30cm) of length.
Close, then pass the yarn through the tomato from bottom to top and bring the yarn out through the starting magic circle. Pull on the yarn to flatten the tomato a bit and to give it the desired shape. The cone formed by the first 3 rnds must be pushed back to the inside of the tomato to form a little hollow. Take another stitch with the yarn to secure it, and then clip it.

STALK

Work in green using the smaller crochet hook.
Rnd 1: 5 sc in 1 magic circle (5 st).
Rnds 2 and 3: 5 sc (5 st).
Rnd 4: 1 sl st in the **front loop only**, (5 ch, 1 sc in the 2nd st from the hook, then continuing along the chain: 1 sl st, 2 sc; 1 sl st in the **front loop only** of the next st of rnd 3) x 5. The 5th time, make the last sl st in the 1st st of rnd 3, above the 1st st of rnd 4. Cut the yarn, leaving 20in. (50cm) of length.

ASSEMBLY

Sew the stalk to the middle of the tomato, on the same side as the starting magic circle. Sew around the central stem, leaving the leaves of the stalk free. Pass the yarn through the tomato, from top to bottom, and with this same yarn, embroider 5 small lines in a star around the last rnd of the tomato. Pull the yarn to the inside.

Eggplant

Dimensions
Diameter: 2in. (5 cm)
Height: 4in. (10 cm)

Important:
The eggplant is crocheted in a spiral. The stem is crocheted along a starting chain. The stalk is crocheted first in a spiral, and then in rows to form the points.

Material
› 1 crochet hook, size C-2 or D-3 (3mm)
› DMC Natura Medium Just Cotton (1¾oz.–82yds.) (50g–75m), shade 126, violet, ¾oz. (20g); shade 198, green, ⅛oz. (5g).

STEM

Work in green.
Make a chain of 5 ch, leaving 4in. (10cm) of yarn at the start. 1 sl st in the 2nd st from the hook, 3 sl st along the chain.
Cut the yarn, leaving 4in. of length.

STALK

Work in green.
Rnd 1: 6 sc in a magic circle. Do not cut the starting yarn. (6 st).
Rnd 2: 6 inc (12 st).
Rnd 3: (1 sc, 1 inc) x 6 (18 st).
Rnd 4: (1 sc, 1 inc, 1 sc) x 6 (24 st).
Continue with the same yarn, crocheting the following in rows.
Row 1: 5 sc, 1 ch (5 st).
Row 2: Turn the work, skip the 1st st, 4 sc, 1 ch (4 st).
Row 3: Turn, skip the 1st st, 3 sc, 1 ch (3 st).
Row 4: Turn, skip the 1st st, 2 sc, 1 ch (2 st).

Row 5: Turn, 1 ch, 1 sc in the 2nd st from the hook (last ch of row 4), skip 1 st, 1 sc in the following st (on row 4). Crochet 3 sc on the edge of the triangle formed by rows 1 to 5 to go back down to the next st on rnd 4. Make 1 sl st in this st (6th st of rnd 4).

Repeat rows 1 to 5 three more times to form 4 points on the stalk of the eggplant. The 2nd point ends with 1 sl st in the 12th st of rnd 4, the 3rd point ends in the 18th st, and the 4th point ends in the 24th st.

Cut the yarn, leaving 28in. (70cm) of length.

EGGPLANT

Work in violet.
Rnd 1: 6 sc in a magic circle (6 st).
Rnd 2: 6 inc (12 st).
Rnd 3: (1 sc, 1 inc) x 6 (18 st).
Rnd 4: (1 sc, 1 inc, 1 sc) x 6 (24 st).
Rnd 5: (7 sc, 1 inc) x 3 (27 st).
Rnd 6: (3 sc, 1 inc, 5 sc) x 3 (30 st).
Rnd 7: (7 sc, 1 inc, 2 sc) x 3 (33 st).
Rnds 8 to 12: 33 sc (33 st).
Rnd 13: 15 sc, (2 sc, 1 dec, 2 sc) x 3 (30 st).
Rnds 14 and 15: 30 sc (30 st).
Rnd 16: 15 sc, (3 sc, 1 dec) x 3 (27 st).
Rnds 17 and 18: 27 sc (27 st).
Rnd 19: (7 sc, 1 dec) x 3 (24 st)
Rnds 20 and 21: 24 sc (24 st).
Rnd 22: (3 sc, 1 dec, 3 sc) x 3 (21 st).
Start stuffing.
Rnd 23: (5 sc, 1 dec) x 3 (18 st).
Rnd 24: (1 sc, 1 dec) x 6 (12 st).
Finish stuffing.
Rnd 25: 6 dec (6 st).
Close and bring the yarn to the inside.

ASSEMBLY

Sew the stem to the stalk by passing the yarns of the stem through the magic circle and tying them on the back side with the starting yarn of the stalk. Using the green yarn of the stalk, sew the stalk to the top of the eggplant.

Peas

Dimensions
Length: 3⅓in. (8.5cm)

Important:
The peas are crocheted in a spiral. The pod is crocheted around a starting chain, to form an oval.
The stem is crocheted along a starting chain.

Material
›   1 crochet hook, size B-1 or C-2 (2.5mm)
›   DMC Natura Just Cotton (1¾oz.–170yds.) (50g–155m), shade 76, light green, 11yds. (10m), and shade 48, dark green, 11yds. (10m)

PEAS × 4

Work in light green.
Rnd 1: 6 sc in 1 magic circle (6 st).
Rnd 2: 6 inc (12 st).
Rnds 3 and 4: 12 sc (12 st).
Rnd 5: 6 dec (6 st).
Stuff firmly. Close and pull the yarn to the inside.

POD

Work in dark green.
Rnd 1: Make a chain of 18 ch, 1 sc in the 2nd st from the hook (mark this st as the 1st st of the rnd), 15 sc along the chain, 3 sc in the last st of the chain, then coming back up the other side of the chain: 15 sc, 1 inc in the last st (36 st).
Rnd 2: 1 inc, 15 sc, 1 inc, 1 sc, 1 inc, 15 sc, 1 inc, 1 sc (40 st).
Rnd 3: 1 inc, 17 sc, 3 inc, 17 sc, 2 inc (46 st).
Rnd 4: 21 sc, 2 inc, 21 sc, 2 inc (50 sc).
Rnd 5: 50 sc (50 st).
Rnd 6: 48 sc, 1 sl st. Flatten the pod so that this 49th st is at one end.

The last st of the rnd will be made by crocheting the 2 thicknesses together: insert the crochet hook in the following st (the 50th st of rnd 5) and in the preceding st (the 48th st of rnd 6, from the back to the front) and make 1 sl st (50 st).

Rnd 7: Make 2 other sl st by crocheting the 2 thicknesses together; continue by crocheting a single thickness of the pod: 18 sl st, 3 sc, 1 sl st; once again crochet the 2 thicknesses together: insert the crochet hook in the following st (the 25th of rnd 6) and in the preceding one (the 23rd of rnd 7, from the back to the front) and make 1 sl st; make 2 additional sl st in this manner; finish the rnd by crocheting a single thickness of the pod: 18 sl st. Stop the yarn on the back of the pod.

STEM

Work in dark green. The explanations are broken down into 3 parts; you must crochet them in order using the same yarn.
Leave 6in. (15cm) of yarn at the start before the slip knot.

1st Leaf
Make a chain of 7 ch, 1 sl st in the 2nd st from the hook, then continue along the chain: 1 sc, 2 hdc, 1 sc, 1 sl st.

Stem
5 ch, 1 sc in the 2nd st from the hook, then continue along the chain: 3 sl st; 1 sl st in the starting st of the chain for the 1st leaf (at the level of the slip knot).

2nd Leaf
6 ch, 1 sl st in the 2nd st from the crochet hook, then continue along the chain: 1 sc, 2 hdc, 1 sc; 1 sl st in the starting st of the chain for the 1st leaf. Cut the yarn, leaving 8in. (20cm) for sewing.

ASSEMBLY

Sew the stem to one end of the pod.
It must be lined up with the pod, and the top of each leaf must be sewn on the side.
Bring the yarn to the inside and tuck in the yarn.

IMPORTANT!

If the peas are intended for a child younger than 3 years old, make sure to attach all 4 peas securely to avoid the risk of choking.

Using a long needle and a light green yarn, pass through the center of each pea. Make several stitches to attach each pea securely.

Avocado Half

Dimensions
Diameter: 2⅛in. (5.5cm)
Length: 3⅛in. (8cm)

Important:
All the pieces are crocheted in a spiral.

Material
› 1 crochet hook, size C-2 or D-3 (3mm)
› DMC Natura Medium Just Cotton (1¾oz.–82yds.) (50g–75m), shade 198, light green, ⅛oz. (4g); shade 138, green, ⅓oz. (10g), and shade 11, taupe, 3¼yd. (3m)

SLICE

Work in taupe.
Rnd 1: 5 sc in a magic circle (5 st).
Rnd 2: 5 inc (10 st).
Rnd 3: (2 sc, 1 inc, 2 sc) x 2 (12 st).
Rnd 4: (1 sc, 1 inc, 1 sc) x 3 (15 st).
In light green.
Tie the taupe and green yarns together after the change of color; cut the taupe yarn, keeping 8in. (20cm) of length.
Rnd 5: In the **front loop only**: (1 sc, 1 inc, 1 sc) x 2, 2 sc; 6 ch, 1 sc in the 2nd st from the hook, 4 sc coming back down the length of the chain; 1 sc on rnd 4, in the same st as the 10th st of rnd 5, 1 sc, (1 sc, 1 inc, 1 sc) x 2 (30 st).
Rnd 6: (1 sc, 1 inc, 1 sc) x 2, 2 sc, 3 hdc, 3 sc, 2 inc, 3 sc, 3 hdc, 2 sc, (1 sc, 1 inc, 1 sc) x 2 (36 st).
Rnd 7: (1 inc, 3 sc) x 2, 2 sc, 5 hdc, 2 sc, 2 inc, 3 sc, 5 hdc, 1 sc, (3 sc, 1 inc) x 2. Mark the last st of the rnd. (42 st).
Rnd 8: 1 sl st, do not crochet the other st of the rnd (42 st).
Close invisibly. Stuff the seed; then, with the remaining taupe yarn, take several stitches across the edge of the seed to hold the stuffing inside.

SKIN

Work in green.
Rnd 1: 6 sc in a magic circle (6 st).
Rnd 2: 6 inc (12 st).
Rnd 3: (1 sc, 1 inc) x 6 (18 st).
Rnd 4: 7 sc, 1 inc, 1 sc; 6 ch, 1 sc in the 2nd st from the hook, 4 sc coming back down the length of the chain; 1 sc on rnd 3, in the same st as the 10th st of rnd 4, 1 inc, 8 sc (31 st).
Rnd 5: 1 sc, 1 inc, 7 sc, 3 hdc, 2 sc, 2 inc, 2 sc, 3 hdc, 7 sc, 1 inc, 2 sc (35 st).
Rnd 6: (1 inc, 3 sc) x 2, 1 sc, 5 hdc, 2 sc, 2 inc, 3 sc, 5 hdc, (3 sc, 1 inc) x 2, 1 sc (41 st).
Rnd 7: 40 sc, 1 inc (42 st).
Rnd 8: (2 sc, 1 inc, 2 sc) x 2, 8 sc, 4 inc, 8 sc, (2 sc, 1 inc, 2 sc) x 2, 2 sc (50 st). Do not cut the yarn.

ASSEMBLY

Crochet the two parts together edge to edge to assemble them.
Continuing with the green yarn, insert the crochet hook in the 1st st of rnd 8 of the skin, and then in the previously marked st on the slice, **from back to front**, and make 1 sc.
Continue in the same way all around: 2 sc; 1 sc by inserting the hook in the following st of the skin and **in the same st** of the slice as the preceding st; 5 sc; 1 sc by inserting in the following st of the skin and **in the same st** of the slice as the preceding st; 10 sc; (1 sc, 1 sc by inserting the hook in the following st of the skin and **in the same st** of the slice as the preceding st) x 4; 11 sc; 1 sc by inserting the hook in the following st of the skin and **in the same st** of the slice as the preceding st. Start to stuff; 5 sc; 1 sc by inserting the hook in the following st of the skin and **in the same st** of the slice as the preceding st; finish stuffing; 3 sc, 1 sl st.
Close invisibly, and pull the yarn to the inside.

Carrot

Dimensions
Length: 5½in. (14cm)

Important:
The carrot is crocheted in a spiral. The carrot top is crocheted along a starting chain.

Material
› 2 crochet hooks, size B-1 or C-2 (2.5mm), and size C-2 or D-3 (3mm)
› DMC Natura Medium Just Cotton (1¾oz.–82yds.) (50g–75m), shade 109, orange, ⅓oz. (10g)
› DMC Natura Just Cotton (1¾oz.–170yds.) (50g–155m), shade 13, green, 5½yds. (5m)

CARROT TOP × 3

Work in green using the smaller crochet hook. Leave 4in. (10cm) of yarn at the start, before the slip knot.

Leaf 1
Make a chain of 13 ch, 1 sl st in the 2nd st from the hook, 3 sl st continuing along the chain.

Leaf 2
5 ch, 1 sl st in the 2nd st from the hook, 2 sl st continuing along the chain.

Leaf 3
4 ch, 1 sl st in the 2nd st from the hook, 2 sl st continuing along the chain, 1 sl st in the 1 st ch of leaf 2.

Leaf 4
5 ch, 1 sl st in the 2nd st from the hook, 3 sl st continuing along the chain, 1 sl st in the 8th sl st of the starting chain of leaf 1, 1 sl st in the following st.

Leaf 5

8 ch, 1 sl st in the 2nd st from the hook, 4 sl st continuing along the chain.

Leaf 6
5 ch, 1 sl st in the 2nd st from the hook, 2 sl st continuing along the chain.

Leaf 7
4 ch, 1 sl st in the 2nd st from the hook, 2 sl st continuing along the chain, 1 sl st in the 1 st ch of leaf 6.

Leaf 8
5 ch, 1 sl st in the 2nd st from the hook, 3 sl st continuing along the chain, 1 sl st in the 2nd ch of the starting chain of leaf 5, 1 sl st in the following st. End with 1 sl st in the first 6 st of the starting chain of leaf 1.
Cut the yarn, leaving 4in. of length.

CARROT

Work in orange using the larger crochet hook.
Rnd 1: 6 sc in a magic circle; do not cut the starting yarn (6 st).
Rnd 2: 6 inc (12 st).
Rnd 3: (1 inc, 1 sc) x 6 (18 st).
Rnd 4: (5 sc, 1 inc) x 3 (21 st).
Attach the carrot tops: Bring the 2 yarns of the 1st top through the magic circle and tie them to the starting yarn of the carrot, on the inside, tying them securely. Next bring in the 2 yarns of the 2nd top and tie them to the orange yarn as well. Do the same with the 3rd top. Cut the yarns after everything has been tied.
Rnd 5: 21 sc (21 st).
Rnd 6: (5 sc, 1 dec) x 3 (18 st).
Rnds 7 and 8: 18 sc (18 st).
Rnd 9: (7 sc, 1 dec) x 2 (16 st).
Rnds 10 and 11: 16 sc (16 st).
Rnd 12: (3 sc, 1 dec, 3 sc) x 2 (14 st).
Start stuffing.
Rnds 13 and 14: 14 sc (14 st).
Rnd 15: (5 sc, 1 dec) x 2 (12 st).
Rnd 16: 12 sc (12 st).
Continue to stuff.
Rnd 17: 12 sc (12 st).
Rnd 18: (2 sc, 1 dec, 2 sc) x 2 (10 st).
Rnd 19: 10 sc (10 st).
Continue stuffing, then keep stuffing as you go along until the end.
Rnd 20: 3 sc, 1 dec, 5 sc (9 st).

Rnd 21: 7 sc, 1 dec (8 st).
Rnd 22: 1 sc, 1 dec, 5 sc (7 st).
Rnd 23: 4 sc, 1 dec, 1 sc (6 st).
Rnd 24: 1 dec, 4 sc (5 st).
Close by pulling tight and making a knot, leaving the yarn on the outside. Cut, leaving an inch or so of length for the roots.

Leek

Dimensions
Height: 5½in. (14cm)

Important:
All pieces are crocheted using 2 yarns simultaneously.
The different pieces are crocheted first spirally, then in rows to form the leaves.

Material
› 1 crochet hook, size C-2 or D-3 (3mm)
› DMC Natura Just Cotton (1¾oz.–170yds.) (50g–155m), shade 48, green, ½oz. (15g); shade 89, light green, ⅒oz. (2g); shade 01, white, ⅓oz. (8g)
› DMC Natura Medium Just Cotton (1¾oz.–82yds.) (50g–75m), shade 31, beige, 2¼yds. (2m)

1st INNER LEAF (SMALL)

Work in green.
Rnd 1: 5 sc in magic circle (5 st).
Rnd 2: 5 sc in the **back loop only**.
Mark the front loop of the 1st st of rnd 1. (5 st.).
Rnd 3: 5 sc (5 st)
Rnd 4: 4 sc, 2 ch, do not crochet the last st (5 st).
Continue with the same yarns, crocheting the following in rows.
Row 1: Turn the work and crochet in the 4 crocheted st in rnd 4 and the last st of rnd 3: 1 hdc, 3 sc, 1 hdc, 2 ch (5 st).
Row 2: Turn, 1 hdc, 3 sc, 1 hdc, 2 ch (5 st).
Row 3: Turn, 1 hdc, 3 sc, 1 hdc, 1 ch (5 st).
Rows 4 and 5: Turn, 5 sc, 1 ch (5 st).
Row 6: Turn, 5 sc (5 st).
Make an invisible knot and pull the yarns back in over the length of the st.

2nd INNER LEAF (MEDIUM)

Work in green.

Rnd 1: Insert the crochet hook in the previously marked loop (rnd 1 of the small leaf), from the bottom to the top, and pull 2 green yarns through.

Keep a 16in. (40cm) length of starting yarn.

Make one inc in the same loop, 4 inc in the following **front loops** (10 st).

Rnd 2: 10 sc in the **back loop only**. (10 st).

Rnd 3: 10 sc, 2 ch (10 st).

Continue with the same yarns, crocheting the following in rows.

Row 1: Turn the work and crochet in the 10 crocheted st of rnd 3: 3 hdc, 4 sc, 3 hdc, 2 ch (10 st).

Row 2: Turn, 3 hdc, 4 sc, 3 hdc, 2 ch (10 st).

Row 3: Turn, 3 hdc, 4 sc, 3 hdc, 1 ch (10 st).

Row 4: Turn, 10 sc, 2 ch (10 st).

Row 5: Turn, 10 hdc, 2 ch (10 st).

Row 6: Turn, 10 hdc (10 st).

Make a knot invisibly and work the yarns in over the width of the st.

LEEK

Work in white.

Rnd 1: 6 sc in a magic circle (6 st).

Rnd 2: 6 inc (12 st).

Rnd 3: (1 sc, 1 inc) x 6 (18 st).

Rnd 4: 18 sc (18 st).

Rnd 5: (1 sc, 1 dec) x 6 (12 st).

Cut 10 pieces of beige yarn, 6in. (15cm) each. Fold each one in half and make an overhand knot in the doubled yarn, close to the fold. Thread the 2 ends through a needle and pull them from the inside to the outside of the leek. The knots must remain on the inside of the leek and the 2 ends will remain on the outside, each piece in a different st. Distribute them over the entire end of the leek. Twist apart all the yarns to imitate the roots.

Rnds 6 and 7: 12 sc (12 st).

Start to stuff, then continue stuffing as you go along.

Rnds 8 to 19: 12 sc (12 st).

Continue with 1 white yarn and 1 light green yarn.

Rnds 20 and 21: 12 sc (12 st).

Continue with 2 light green yarns.

Rnd 22: (3 sc, 1 inc) x 3 (15 st).

Rnd 23: 15 sc (15 st).

Continue with 1 light green yarn and 1 green yarn.

Rnd 24: (2 sc, 1 inc, 2 sc) x 3 (18 st)
Continue with 2 green yarns, crocheting in rows.

3rd Leaf
Row 1: 1 sc in the **back loop only**, 4 sc, 1 sc in the **back loop only** (mark the front loop of this st), 3 ch (6 st).
Row 2: Turn the work, 1 sc in the 2nd st from the crochet hook, 1 sc in the next st of the chain, 6 sc, 3 ch (8 st).
Row 3: Turn, 1 sc in the 2nd st from the crochet hook, 1 sc in the next st of the chain, 8 sc, 3 ch (10 st).
Rows 4 and 5: Turn, 1 dc, 1 hdc, 6 sc, 1 hdc, 1 dc, 3 ch (10 st).
Row 6: Turn, 1 dc, 1 hdc, 6 sc, 1 hdc, 1 dc, 2 ch (10 st).
Rows 7 and 8: Turn, 10 hdc, 2 ch (10 st).
Row 9: Turn, 10 hdc (10 st).
Make an invisible knot and work the yarn back in over the width of the st.

4th Leaf
Pull 2 green yarns through the previously-marked st on row 1 of the leek (3rd leaf).
Keep an 8in. (20cm) length of starting yarn.
Row 1: 1 sc in the **front loop of the same st**, 12 sc in the st of rnd 24 of the leek, 1 sc in the **front loop of the 1st st** of row 1 of the leek, 1 ch (14 st).
Row 2: Turn, 14 sc, 2 ch (14 st).
Rows 3 and 4: Turn, 2 hdc, 10 sc, 2 hdc, 2 ch (14 st).
Row 5: Turn, 2 hdc, 10 sc, 2 hdc, 1 ch (14 st).
Row 6: Turn, 14 sc, 2 ch (14 st).

Rows 7 and 8: Turn, 14 hdc, 2 ch (14 st).
Row 9: Turn, 14 hdc. (14 st).
Make an invisible knot and work the yarns back in over the width of the st.

ASSEMBLY

Finish stuffing the leek. Position the 2 inner leaves inside the open leek. With the starting yarn of the middle inner leaf, sew these 2 leaves inside the leek so as to close it. At the same time, sew the ch of rows 1 and 2, which are at the ends of the 3rd leaf, so as to hold them securely in place. Pull the starting yarns of the 4th leaf back inside the work. Finally, cut the roots of the leek to a little less than 1in.

Cauliflower

Dimensions
Height: 2¾in. (7cm)
Diameter: 3½in. (9cm)

Important:
The cauliflower is crocheted in a spiral, the florets in triple crochet.
For each floret, make 4 tr started in the same st and run them together:
—yarn over twice, insert the crochet hook in the indicated st;
—yo a 3rd time and bring the yarn through the st;
—yo a 4th time and bring the yarn back through 2 loops;
—yo a 5th time and bring the yarn back through 2 loops.
Repeat these 4 steps 3 times more in the same st so as to have 4 tr started.
Finally, do 1 last yo and bring the yarn through the 5 loops that are on the hook.
The leaves are crocheted in rows in a U around a starting chain.

Material
›   1 crochet hook, size E-4 (3.5mm)
›   DMC Natura Medium Just Cotton (1¾oz.–82yds.) (50g–75m), shade 01, white, 1oz. (25g)
›   DMC Natura Just Cotton (1¾oz.–170yds.) (50g–155m), shade 13, green, 1oz. (30g)

CAULIFLOWER

Work in white.
Rnd 1: 6 sc in a magic circle (6 st).
Rnd 2: 5 sc, 1 hdc (6 st).
Rnd 3: in the **front loop only**: (1 dc and 1 flore in the same st) x 6 (12 st).
Rnd 4: (1 dc and 1 floret in the same st) x 12 (24 st).
Rnd 5: [1 dc and 1 floret in the same st, (1 dc, 1 floret) x 2, 1 dc, 1 floret and 1 dc in the same st, (1 floret, 1 dc) x 2, 1 floret] x 2 (28 st).
Rnd 6: 1 dc and 1 floret in the same st, (1 dc, 1 floret) x 13, 1 dc (29 st).
Rnd 7: (1 floret, 1 dc) x 14, 1 floret (29 st).

Rnd 8: 1 hdc, 29 sc (29 st).
Rnd 9: 4 sc, (1 dec, 3 sc) x 5 (24 st).
Rnd 10: (1 sc, 1 dec, 1 sc) x 6 (18 st).
Start to stuff.
Rnd 11: (1 sc, 1 dec) x 6 (12 st).
Finish stuffing.
Rnd 12: 6 dec (6 st).
Close and pull the yarn to the inside.

LEAVES × 5

Work in white.
Row 1: make a chain of 13 ch, 1 sc in the 2nd st from the crochet hook; then continuing along the chain: 10 sc; at the end of the chain: 2 sc, change color to green, 3 hdc; from the other side of the chain: 10 hdc (26 st).
Row 2: turn the work, 3 sl st, 2 ch, 1 hdc in the same st, 8 hdc, (2 hdc in 1 st) x 3, 11 hdc (29 st).
Row 3: turn, 3 sl st, 2 ch, 1 hdc in the same st,
8 hdc, (2 hdc in 1 st) x 4, 10 hdc (30 st).
Row 4: turn, 2 sl st, 2 ch, 1 hdc in the same st, 7 hdc, (2 hdc in 1 st, 1 hdc) x 4, 9 hdc (31 st).
Row 5: turn, 2 sl st, 2 ch, 1 hdc in the same st, 10 hdc, 1 sc, 1 sl st.
Do not crochet the following st.
Cut the yarns, leaving 24in. (60cm) of length.
Thread the starting and changing yarns under a few st before cutting them off, even with the work.

ASSEMBLY

Position the 5 leaves around the cauliflower, overlapping them at the base and using pins to keep them in place. Use the yarns at the end of each leaf to sew the bottom 2 tiers of the leaves to the cauliflower. Leave the points of the leaves free.

Radish

Dimensions
Diameter: 1⅛in. (3cm)
Length: 3½in. (9cm)
(leaves included)

Important:
The radish is crocheted in a spiral, using 2 yarns at the same time. The leaves are crocheted around a base chain, using a single yarn.

Material
› 2 crochet hooks, size B-1 or C-2 (2.5mm) and size C-2 or D-3 (3mm)
› DMC Natura Just Cotton (1¾oz.–170yds.) (50g–155m), shade 13, green, 6½yds. (6m); shade 61, rose, ⅒oz. (2g); shade 01, white, ⅒oz. (2g)

LEAF × 3

Work in green, using the smaller crochet hook.
Make a chain of 6 ch, keeping 6in. (15cm) of starting yarn.
Rnd 1: 1 sc in the 2nd ch from the crochet hook, 3 hdc; in the st at the end of the chain: 4 hdc; crocheting on the other side of the chain: 3 hdc, 1 inc (13 st).
Rnd 2: 1 sc, (3 ch, 1 sl st in the next st of rnd 1) x 12.
End by making 1 sc in the 1st st of rnd 2 and 9 ch.
Cut the yarn, leaving 4in. (10cm) of length.
Using a needle, pull the starting yarn under the stitches of rnd 1 and cut it off even with the work.

RADISH

Work in rose, using 2 yarns and the larger crochet hook.
Rnd 1: 6 sc in a magic circle.
Do not cut the starting yarn. (6 st).
Rnd 2: 6 inc (12 st).
Rnd 3: (1 sc, 1 inc) x 6 (18 st).
Rnds 4 to 6: 18 sc (18 st).

Using a needle, bring the starting yarns of the leaves through the starting magic circle and tie them to the starting yarn of the radish. Continue with 1 rose yarn and 1 white yarn.

Rnd 7: (2 sc, 1 dec, 2 sc) x 3 (15 st).

Using 2 white yarns.

Rnd 8: (3 sc, 1 dec) x 3 (12 st).

Start to stuff.

Rnd 9: 6 dec (6 st).

Finish stuffing and cut the yarns, leaving 6in. (15cm) of length. Close and tighten well.

Do not bring the yarns to the inside, but make a secure knot close to the surface of the radish. Cut the yarns to about 1in. (2cm) and twist them apart to make roots.

Button Mushroom

Dimensions
Diameter: 2in. (5cm)
Height: 1½in. (4cm)

Important:
All pieces are crocheted in a spiral.
The mushroom cap can be made in off white or taupe.

Material
› 1 crochet hook, size C-2 or D-3 (3mm)
› DMC Natura Medium Just Cotton (1¾oz.–82yds.) (50g–75m), shade 03, off white/shade 11, taupe, ⅓oz. (10g)

STEM

Work in off white.
Rnd 1: 5 sc in a magic circle (5 st).
Rnd 2: 5 inc (10 st).
Rnd 3: 10 sc in the **back loop only** (10 st).
Rnds 4 and 5: 10 sc (10 st).
Rnd 6: 10 inc in the **front loop only** (20 st).
Rnd 7: 1 sl st, do not crochet the other st of the rnd (20 st).
Cut the yarn, leaving 12in. (30cm) of length. Stuff the stem.

CAP

Work in off white or taupe.
Rnd 1: 6 sc in a magic circle (6 st).
Rnd 2: 6 inc (12 st).
Rnd 3: (1 sc, 1 inc) x 6 (18 st).
Rnd 4: (1 sc, 1 inc, 1 sc) x 6 (24 st).
Rnd 5: (7 sc, 1 inc) x 3 (27 st).
Rnd 6: (3 sc, 1 inc, 5 sc) x 3 (30 st).
Rnds 7 and 8: 30 sc (30 st).

Rnd 9: (1 dec, 1 sc) x 9, 1 dec, 1 sl st (20 st).
End the yarn in an invisible way and stuff the cap.

ASSEMBLY

Sew the stem to the cap as follows: insert the crochet hook in the next st of the stem, from the outside to the inside, and then in the back loop of a st of the cap (the loop that is toward the inside of the cap), from the inside to the outside. By inserting the hook in this way, the edges of the stem and the cap will be positioned back to back. Continue in that manner all around and then bring the yarn to the inside and cut it close to the surface of the work.

Pumpkin

⏱ 2 hrs. 30 min.

Dimensions
Diameter: 3in. (8cm)
Height: 2⅛in. (5.5cm)

Important:
The pumpkin is crocheted in a spiral. Make sure to crochet in the back loop only when indicated. The stitches for which this instruction is not given must be crocheted normally, in both loops. The leaf is crocheted in rows, turning the work at the end of each row.

Material
› 2 crochet hooks, size B-1 or C-2 (2.5mm) and size C-2 or D-3 (3mm)
› DMC Natura Medium Just Cotton (1¾oz.–82yds.) (50g–75m), shade 109, orange, 1oz. (30g); shade 89, chestnut brown, 2¼yds. (2m), and shade 198, light green, ⅒oz. (2g)
› DMC Natura Just Cotton (1¾oz.–170yds.) (50g–155m), shade 13, green, ⅒oz. (2g)

PUMPKIN

Work in chestnut brown, using the larger crochet hook.
Rnd 1: 6 sc in a magic circle (6 st).
Rnd 2: 6 inc (12 st).
In orange.
Rnd 3: in the back loop only: (1 sc, 1 inc) x 6 (18 st).
Rnd 4: (1 sc in the back loop only, 1 inc, 1 sc) x 6 (24 st).
Rnd 5: (1 sc in the back loop only, 2 sc, 1 inc) x 6 (30 st).
Rnd 6: (1 sc in the back loop only, 1 sc, 1 inc, 2 sc) x 6 (36 st).
Rnd 7: (1 sc in the back loop only, 4 sc, 1 inc) x 6 (42 st).
Rnd 8: (1 sc in the back loop only, 2 sc, 1 inc, 3 sc) x 6 (48 st).
Rnd 9: (1 sc in the back loop only, 6 sc, 1 inc) x 6 (54 st).
Rnds 10 to 18: (1 sc in the back loop only, 8 sc) x 6 (54 st).
Rnd 19: (1 sc in the back loop only, 1 dec, 6 sc) x 6 (48 st).
Rnd 20: (1 sc in the back loop only, 2 sc, 1 dec, 3 sc) x 6 (42 st).

Rnd 21: (1 sc in the back loop only, 4 sc, 1 dec) x 6 (36 st).
Rnd 22: (1 sc in the back loop only, 1 dec, 3 sc) x 6 (30 st).
Rnd 23: (1 sc in the back loop only, 1 sc, 1 dec, 1 sc) x 6 (24 st).
Stuff the pumpkin lightly. It should have enough stuffing so that it is well rounded, but with enough slack so that you will be able to tighten each section later.
Rnd 24: (1 sc in the back loop only, 1 sc, 1 dec) x 6 (18 st).
Work in light green.
When making the color change, keep the orange yarn toward the outside of the pumpkin and cut it, keeping 52in. (130cm) of length.
Tie a knot behind the green starting yarn.
Rnd 25: (1 sc in the back loop only, 1 sc, run 2 st together) x 6 (12 st).
For more instructions on how to run 2 st together, see the "Techniques" chapter,
Rnd 26: 12 sc (12 st).
Rnd 27: (1 sc, 1 dec, 1 sc) x 3 (9 st).
Rnd 28: (1 sc, 1 dec) x 3 (6 st).
Rnd 29: 6 sc (6 st).
Before finishing crocheting the stem, shape the pumpkin. Using a needle with the orange yarn set aside, insert the needle in the back loop of the 1st st of rnd 24, from the outside to the inside. Go across the pumpkin from top to bottom, bringing the needle out again between the 1st st of rounds 2 and 3 (where the chestnut brown changes to orange). Then pass the yarn under the front loops of the 1st st of rounds 3 to 24, and tighten the yarn to form the start of the 1st section of the pumpkin.
Insert the needle at the same spot on the top of the pumpkin, bringing it out this time at the bottom of the section, following the front loops, always at the transition from chestnut brown to orange. Pass the yarn under the front loops over the entire height of the pumpkin, as before, and tighten the yarn well. Continue as described for the other 4 columns of front loops to form 6 sections. Take several stitches at the top and bottom to secure the yarn and to even out the height of the pumpkin, if necessary. Clip the yarn evenly with the surface of the pumpkin.
Stuff the stem lightly and close by inserting the hook into the back loops of the last 6 st, from the inside toward the outside. Pull the yarn inside and cut it off even with the surface.

LEAF

Work in green with the smaller crochet hook.
<u>1st part</u>

Row 1: Make a chain of 7 ch, 1 sc in the 3rd st from the crochet hook; continuing along the chain: 3 sc; in the st at the end of the chain: (1 sc, 3 ch, 1 sc); on the other side of the chain: 4 sc (13 st).
Row 2: Turn the work, skip 1 st, 1 sl st in the next st, 2 ch, 3 sc in the back loop only; insert the crochet hook in the hole formed by the 3-ch chain of the preceding row: 1 sc, 4 ch, 1 sc; 4 sc in the back loop only. (14 st).
Row 3: turn, 2 ch, 5 sc; inserting the crochet hook in the hole formed by the chain of the preceding row: 1 sc, 4 ch, 1 sc; 4 sc (15 st).
Row 4: turn, skip 1 st, 1 sl st in the next st, 2 ch, 3 sc in the back loop only; inserting the crochet hook in the hole formed by the chain of the preceding row: 2 sc, 3 ch, 2 sc; 5 sc in the back loop only. (16 st).
Row 5: turn, 2 ch, 7 sc; insert the crochet hook in the hole formed by the chain of the preceding row: 3 sc (mark the 2nd sc); 5 sc (15 st).

Tie a subtle knot in the yarn and pass it under some st of row 5. Clip close to the surface of the work. Also pass the starting yarn under a few st before cutting it.

2nd part
Make a chain of 25 ch, keeping 6in. (15cm) of starting yarn, 1 sc in the 2nd st from the hook, 23 sc along the chain, finish with 1 sl st by inserting the hook in the st marked on the 1 st part and in the last ch of the chain.
Cut the yarn, leaving 6in. (15cm) of length.

Attach the leaf at the base of the green stem of the pumpkin with the starting and ending yarns.

Printed in Great Britain
by Amazon

43498368R00064